The Zen of Cricket

The
ZEN OF CRICKET
Learning from Positive Thought

TONY FRANCIS

Stanley Paul
LONDON

Stanley Paul & Co. Ltd

An imprint of the Random Century Group
20 Vauxhall Bridge Road, London SW1V 2SA

Random Century Australia (Pty) Ltd
20 Alfred Street, Milsons Point, Sydney, NSW 2061

Random Century New Zealand Ltd
191 Archers Road, PO Box 40–086, Auckland 10

Random Century South Africa (Pty) Ltd
PO Box 337, Bergvlei 2012, South Africa

First published 1992
Copyright © Tony Francis 1992

The right of Tony Francis to be identified as the author of
this work has been asserted by him in accordance with
the Copyright, Designs and Patents Act, 1988

Set in 11/13pt Sabon by
Deltatype Ltd, Ellesmere Port, Cheshire

Printed and bound in Great Britain by
MacKays of Chatham PLC, Chatham, Kent

A catalogue record for this book is available upon
request from the British Library

ISBN 0 09 174648 5

ACKNOWLEDGEMENTS

Thanks are due to the following for allowing use of
copyright photographs as indicated: AllSport (Lloyd,
Thomson, Gavaskar); Patrick Eagar (Gooch, Close,
Lillee, Marshall, Massie, Willis, Steele); Hulton-Deutsch
Picture Library (Miller); Graham Morris (Smith,
Gatting, Richards); Press Association (Ramadhin).

Contents

The Chronicle

1981	Botham beats Australia 3–1 (with a little help from Willis).
1984 and 1986	England 'blackwashed' twice: Gower as well as can be expected!
1990	Hadlee first man past 400 Test wickets; is knighted and retires.
1991	Front page news – England win a Test in the Caribbean for the first time in 22 years.
1991	Hadlee has by-pass surgery.
1992	Gooch's innings of the century: England draw the series against West Indies; so there *is* an answer.

ONE
The Adventure

'He has to live his life, he is not lived by it.
He is in nature, yet he transcends nature.'
ERICH FROMM

Once upon a time, a shepherd boy cheerily rolled a ball of knotted wool along the ground. It was hit across the meadow by another shepherd boy wielding a crook. They could not have known that such a trivial contest would beget the most richly rewarding game in the world. More than a game, of course: a science, a spiritual experience, a religion, a passport to the world and, for thousands upon thousands, a dizzy love affair. Yet cricket is also an anachronism, a glorious irrelevance. No way for twenty-two grown men and two more in white coats to earn their living, cocooned from the commercial and industrial realities of the world around them.

If *playing* was wasteful, what about the ne'er-do-wells who gathered to watch? As early as 1743, *The Gentleman's Magazine* published the following indictment: 'Cricket is certainly a very innocent and wholesome exercise yet it may be absurd if either great or little people make it their business. It is grossly abused when it is made the subject of public advertisement to draw together great crowds of people who ought, all of them, to be somewhere else . . . It propagates a spirit of idleness at a juncture when, with the utmost industry, our debts, taxes and decay of trade will scarce allow us to get bread.'

By the time of the 1850 Factory Act, which gave the working men of Britain Saturday afternoons off, cricket had become the major spectator sport. No longer was it absurd for anyone to make it their business. The professionals were here. They were typified by William Clarke, a streetwise entrepreneur from Nottingham who married the owner of the Trent Bridge Inn and stupefied the locals by slapping an admission charge on the meadow at the back where Nottinghamians were accustomed to enjoying their cricket *gratis*.

Today, upwards of 100,000 spectators a day will flock to see a Test match in Calcutta. Bombay and Melbourne are not far behind. Ian

Botham made his fortune at the game; BSkyB paid a fortune for exclusive access; yet the unconverted remain perplexed. How can you spend five days playing a game that can end without a result they ask. How can you waste five days watching it? It will never make prime-time television in the USA. Football, tennis, boxing, athletics are all international currencies, but cricket, while it thrives in outposts as diverse as Italy and The Netherlands, is a peculiarly English pastime. Therein is its attraction for those of us who despair of proselytizing; who appreciate as only an Englishman can the caress of willow on leather, the scent of a freshly mown outfield, the peel of distant church bells, the plumpness of home-made cakes and the camaraderie as evening shadows lengthen. Then there is the local tavern to round off the day – quaffing ale and offering a dozen excuses for our incompetence; the result of the match submerged by the individual duels which often seem more important. Whoever said cricket was a team game? Is it not really a game for individuals who agree to pool their rewards and share their setbacks? If there is a lonelier man in the game than the fielder who spills a catch or the bowler at the start of his run-up, it is the receiving batsman. He is the most solitary and outnumbered individual in sport, ambushed by eleven opponents bent on his downfall. His colleague at the non- striker's end can do nothing to help.

Everyone who has played cricket knows that feeling. At the highest level it is the supreme test of mind over matter. A batsman opening the innings or facing a crisis must perforce wrest the initiative back from the bowler or ensure that it does not pass to him in the first place. In the last analysis, against the world's fastest bowlers, it may come down to little more than a reflex action. In between deliveries, however, there is time, and that can be an enemy as well as a friend. Erich Fromm says in his book *Psycho-Analysis and Zen Buddhism*: '[man] has awareness of himself, and this awareness of himself as a separate entity makes him feel unbearably alone, lost, powerless.'

The good news is that a batsman who triumphs in this unequal struggle enjoys an unsurpassable sense of power and elation. How the balance of power shifts between batsman and bowler and to what extent the power of positive thought has dictated events in Test match cricket over the last six decades, is largely the subject of this study.

We begin with the eccentrics of the modern era. The crowd-pullers who refused to accept that anything was impossible and inflicted their personalities on cricket to such an extent that their strongest adversaries either buckled at the knees, or struggled to find an adequate response. They 'made things happen', in a phrase – disturbed the flow before it flushed them away; created situations which had no right to exist.

The outstanding example was at Headingley in 1981 when Kim Hughes, the Australian captain, was left clutching defeat instead of victory because Botham 'made something happen'. Technically Botham's was not a good innings and 'Beefy' has always said so. From Australia's point of view it was a dreadful affair. Botham's almighty presence blinded them to the truth – that he was throwing the bat at anything that came along in classic 'do or die' style. Hughes appeared to give no thought to field placings as boundaries flew over the heads of the four slips and gully he steadfastly declined to move. Botham panicked the bowlers, especially Lillee and Geoff Lawson, as impossible began to look more and more possible for reasons which defied logic. It was an instance where a captain's rationality deserted him because his mind could not accept the events his eyes were witnessing. England had followed on 227 behind in the third Test of a series which Australia were already winning 1–0. Several international careers were on the line at a distressingly low point in England's cricket history. Not least of these was Botham's. The captaincy had never sat easily on his shoulders. It was removed after the second Test. Carefree once more, Botham scored a swift 50 in the first innings at Headingley and took six Australian wickets. Some people need to be shorn of responsibility and handed a free role before they can function. Beefy was such a person. Hughes might have guessed something was afoot when both teams checked out of their hotels that Monday morning anticipating an Australian walkover, and Ladbrokes offered 500–1 against an England win. It seemed too cut and dried, and it was.

A stronger captain than Hughes (Benaud, Simpson, Chappell) might have recovered his equilibrium in time. Might have realized there was more chance of catching the whirlwind by deploying Ray Bright, his left-arm spinner, who was forced to stand by for four and a half hours while the pacemen kept feeding Botham (and Dilley) exactly what they wanted. There again, a lesser mortal than Botham would not have relieved Hughes of his senses and could not have contrived such an audacious denouement. Brearley, who had been reinstated as captain in the hope that he could inspire a measure of self-belief into a ragged outfit, is modest enough to disclaim the credit for what happened. His guru-like presence no doubt had a fortifying effect on Botham, whom he watched alfresco at the start of that astonishing innings.

'He tried to force Lillee off the back foot and missed. He looked up to the players' balcony and saw me. I grinned broadly and gestured that he should have tried to hit it even harder, thereby conveying, I hoped, my pleasure at his uninhibited approach and an unqualified approval of his continuing in an extravagant vein.'

Almost a father-and-son relationship. That being the case, Botham had at least three fathers – the real one, Brearley and Brian Close who had watched over his fledgling days at Somerset and counselled fervently against his appointment as England's leader:

'I virtually brought Ian up. Knew him as though he was my own flesh and blood. He didn't even know why things were happening for him the way they did, so what on earth was he going to know about other players? "Both" was slightly immature in the development of his mind. He was just playing games and having a ball. I argued for a month that we shouldn't accept Brearley's recommendation but the chairman of selectors [Alec Bedser] was anxious not to upset Mike because the outgoing captain was a good friend of Gubby Allen.

'When I was outvoted I went into the dressing-room to see Ian. He'd been chosen to captain MCC against West Indies, which was like the half-way stage. I told him, "For Christ's sake don't do the bloody job. It'll come to you in time but you're not ready for it now. Brearley hasn't seen one player improve under his regime in the last two and a half years. He's leaving you a team of no-hopers. Nobody in their right mind would take this job with two series against the West Indies coming up. Why do you think Mike's getting out?" It was no good. They'd dangled the carrot. I couldn't stop him.'

But twelve months against the West Indies and a distressing start to the Australian tour that summer of 1981 *did* stop him. And at Headingley the giant re-awoke. Bob Willis was to apply the *coup de grâce* the following day (we shall look at his rehabilitation in a later chapter), but remarkable as Willis's bowling was, Botham's 'Roy of the Rovers' antics had changed the course of cricket history. I was delighted and privileged to report the news of England's improbable 18-run victory for the 5.45 news on ITN. It is the only time cricket has led the national news bulletin. Everyone was talking about it – the definition of a top story.

Botham's adventure continued. England turned a 0–1 deficit into a 3–1 series success, and schoolboys will be told down the years how one man's magic made it all possible. Australia should have been cruising to victory in a dreary fourth Test at Edgbaston. Botham had been bowling too short, but Brearley tossed him the ball again, more in hope than judgement. Ian decided to pitch it up, nothing more sophisticated than that. It began to swing around a bit. He describes it as 'one of the most ordinary pieces of bowling of all time', but Hughes and company went to pieces again, playing horrific shots, practically queuing up to get back into the pavilion as though an extra-terrestrial force was at play.

From ITN's rooftop cabin we had the same impression. Botham seemed to be plodding up in reasonably benign fashion until wickets began to tumble. He polished off the last five batsmen for one run in 29 balls. Not bad for someone who did not fancy bowling that day.

The fairy tale was completed at Old Trafford where Botham played an infinitely better innings than he did at Headingley, accelerating from three to 103 in 56 balls as Alderman and Lillee (especially) came in for some murderous treatment. Again there had been no hint of what was to come. He was out for a duck in the first innings though he had taken 3–20 including the wicket of Border. In the second innings, once Lillee took the new ball, Beefy was galvanized, smiting the legendary paceman for three 6s in two overs despite the posting of two long legs who could only watch the ball sailing over their heads. More than one hook came off the splice of Botham's bat, testimony to the power of his blows and the courage of his attack. He was without a helmet. His 100 came off 86 balls and contained six 6s – a record for any Test innings in England.

What are we to make of that summer? Botham would say he simply went out and gave it a whirl, but he would be doing himself an injustice. Terry Alderman took 42 wickets in the series, troubling everyone, Gooch in particular; Dennis Lillee, admittedly in the twilight of his career, was still an exceptional performer. Botham made them look prosaic medium-pacers as much by the strength of his personality as the technicalities of his batting. He could have been playing with a railway sleeper! Twelve months of personal misery were blown away in that period between July and August as confidence flooded back. He believed he could move mountains, and he did. The enemy was eating out of his hand because they were transfixed and quite unable to contrive a sane answer.

Botham has been accused of taking more wickets with bad balls than any other Test bowler, but what is a bad ball? Because of his ability to move it both ways batsmen were on edge when they faced him, and he sensed it; knew he was in control; knew he could experiment and have a good chance of escaping punishment. Time and again the pent-up opponent would launch himself at a long-hop or a wide one instead of being content to tuck it away for a single. Making the sudden change from defensive to ultra-offensive is one of the hardest things to do as a batsman, which is why they perished. Bowling, like batting, was an adventure to Beefy. He did not care about giving away a few runs here and there in the quest for something unexpected. Too many medium-pacers have earned their corn from negative bowling just short of a length, tying the batsman down. How much more successful Mike Hendrick would have been with some of Botham's devil. Match-winning medium-pacers are a rarity. Botham was special. The mortals alongside whom he played at his peak, though, were only too eager to inflate his ego, as Close explains.

'Because he was getting so many runs and knocking wickets down and because he was such a big fellah, they encouraged him to be stupid. Not just the media, but the players and the captain as well. It was all bravado – "Come on Both, be Guy the Gorilla" and that sort of thing. He was provoked into thinking the impossible was always possible. When the *Sun* signed him up on the West Indies tour, every other tabloid went hunting for him. He became a dartboard as far as the journalists were concerned. They tried to plant women on him. Let's be honest, when you're a fit young stallion on tour and a smart girl's being paid to make a play for you, how can you refuse?

'Ian hasn't always behaved sensibly but he had to cope with an agent with crazy ideas about selling him in America, not to mention a country which didn't use him properly. He was over-bowled and forced to bat down the order where he had to get on with it. He threw his wicket away so many times instead of getting the chance to build an innings.

'Ordinary people think he's a rogue, but he isn't. If they only met him they'd know. He's matured a lot and his word is his bond. Ian doesn't have a negative thought in his head. That's why the bars empty when he's in action.'

Denis Compton nearly choked on his toast and marmalade when I suggested he came from the same adventure playground as Botham. 'Don't associate me with him! He was overrated. Botham only did well because all the best players had joined Packer. I'd love to have faced him. If you want a world-class all-rounder, Miller's your man, not Botham.'

Yet they were similar in so many ways, principally in their attitude to a game which was the best vehicle for their eccentric talents. Both were footballers too; Compton touched the heights with Arsenal and wartime England while Botham struggled to make the Scunthorpe first team. But then, Denis never appeared in *Jack and the Beanstalk*, nor piloted his own helicopter nor took an elephant across the Alps, although I am sure none of those tasks would have been beyond him. Cricket suited both of them to a T. They loved it and it loved them back. They were united in their (sometimes headstrong) conviction that most opponents were unfit to tie their boots. Whereas the vast majority of cricketers who made a success did so by adapting well to their surroundings, Botham and Compton made their surroundings adapt to *them*. That is surely the essence of greatness and as clear a signal as you could get that sporting prowess is only partly to do with natural ability and textbook coaching. The rest is in the mind. In fact those players who have the strength of character to stray furthest from the recommended ways of doing things – the real adventurers – are the ones who capture our imaginations, show us what the edges of our seats are for.

Compton's insouciance was legendary. Not for him the pacing around a dressing-room or the studying of every ball as he waited to go in. More often than not he would be awoken from a deep slumber, have a bat thrust under his arm and be told he was due at the crease. 'Sometimes I'd forgotten who we were playing,' he confesses. It did not seem to matter. Such was his extraordinary gift that you felt he could be thrown into action anywhere at any time against the best bowlers in the world, with minimal preparation, and still come out on top.

Among his most memorable endeavours was the withering dissection of South Africa's attack at Old Trafford in 1955 when Peter Heine and Neil Adcock were at their most hostile. South Africa, under Jackie McGlew, won that Test to reduce England's lead to 2–1, but not before Compton had cut loose. No less a judge than Colin Cowdrey selects Compton's 158 as the best innings he has seen. And it was preceded by some typical Compton bravado. He could not lay his hand on a suitable bat when the moment arrived, borrowed one at the last minute from Fred Titmus and sauntered out to do battle without a care in the world. Says Cowdrey:

'It was a battered old piece of willow but in Denis's hands it was like a Stradivarius in the hands of Yehudi Menuhin. He simply stroked the ball around the ground, producing every stroke in his vast repertoire, much to the despair of the bowlers. It was a magical innings, full of the unorthodox.'

Denis is proudest of a much earlier innings, again at Old Trafford, while Cowdrey was still at school. The visiting Australians on Sir

Donald Bradman's farewell tour in 1948 are still acknowledged as one of the most powerful outfits in Test history, with Miller and Lindwall spitting fire to head the attack. Attempting to hook a waist-high ball from Lindwall, Compton edged it into his face. He sagged to the ground before being helped off with blood pouring from a gash in his brow. He had scored only 4 and England, already 2–0 down in the series, were in trouble at 32–3. When the fifth wicket tumbled at 119, the wounded hero returned to the middle, only three and a half hours after a doctor had inserted six stitches in his head. Against Lindwall at his most menacing, Denis not only stood firm but improvised his way to an unbeaten 145 which saved the match. In the same series he had withstood Miller and Lindwall in appalling light at Trent Bridge and rescued England from the ignominy of an innings defeat with a titanic contribution of 184. Miller, another adventurer of the same ilk, had incurred the wrath of the crowd by letting go a series of snorting bouncers aimed at Hutton's body. As if the combination of those two was not enough, Compton had to contend with ten stoppages for rain or bad light in a six and a half hour knock spread over three days. Unlike Botham he was not able to change the course of the series (or contemporary history) because the quality of the opposition was hugely superior to Kim Hughes's team, but the thirst for attack even when the odds were stacked against him was equally unquenchable.

'It took me five hours to score 50 in the Trent Bridge Test. I hated every second of it. Defence just didn't come naturally to me. What's the point of letting a bowler dictate to you? If you sit back, he will. Cricket's about stamping your will on the game whether you're batting or bowling. Len Shackleton was an immaculate bowler who could put it on the spot and tie you down for hour after hour if you let him. The thing to do was walk down the wicket to bowlers if there was a danger of being bogged down. Then you'd make them bowl short, lose their rhythm, surrender the initiative.'

Never mind Shackleton; Denis had been known to go down the wicket to Lindwall, which is a bit like trying to catch a bullet in your teeth! The strategy (he would call it natural instinct) did not always come off. He occasionally finished in a heap on the floor, from which position he sometimes had a knack of dispatching the ball to the ropes with that famous late sweep of his. The point is that he was always likely to do something different just for the hell of it. Cricket, even at the highest level was *fun*.

'A happy frame of mind is half the battle. Largely because of the kindness of everyone in my first season in county cricket I could have not felt better towards the world. This outlook, I know, began to show itself in my play.' Denis was writing in his first book, *Playing for England*, published in 1948. Later he talks revealingly about the bowler he most admired and how quickly he realized that a cricketer's mental approach was of paramount importance:

> . . . the best way of allowing a young cricketer to improve his play is not to curtail strokes, no matter how bad they might be according to the copybook, if they produce runs. Even today, after some years in first-class company, I frequently produce strokes that would not win me first prize in any competition – but never forget that *runs* count in cricket.

Bill ('Tiger') O'Reilly was just about the finest bowler in the world when Compton first appeared in an Ashes series fifteen months before the outbreak of World War Two. O'Reilly was thirty-three years of age, Compton just twenty but determined not to be upstaged by the leg-spinner.

> Before sending down his second ball, Bill O'Reilly looked hard at me. I thought for a moment that he was trying to hypnotize me, but obviously the Australian was sizing me up. O'Reilly, first and foremost, was a student of cricket. He studied opposing batsmen with the same care a boxer does a prospective opponent, and if any man had a chink in his defensive armour you can be sure that O'Reilly would spot it. First to last he was an attacking bowler, willing to bowl his heart out rather than give opposing batsmen the impression that they were getting the better of him. In short, the ideal bowler.

After the shock of snicking his first ball just short of slip and denying O'Reilly the joy of capturing the youngster's wicket, Compton moved on to a century, quite clear in his own mind of the route he had to follow. 'Experience had taught me that the way to success in cricket was to make the bowler respect the batsman, not to go out of your way to encourage the man with the ball into thinking he has you worried.'

Keith Miller possessed an infinite capacity to worry any batsman – and a keen sense of timing to go with it. How typical that he should choose Nottingham, the home of Harold Larwood, to unload his bouncers at Hutton. It is interesting that the umpires cautioned the Trent Bridge spectators about excessive barracking, rather than the bowler about intimidatory bowling; you can almost see Miller grinning impishly to himself. Of all Australians since the war, the all-rounder from Melbourne stands head and shoulders above his countrymen when it comes to animal magnetism. No wonder he and Compton have remained close friends for the best part of fifty years. When he stepped into the arena, a shiver of expectancy ran through the crowd. I discovered one of the best evocations in a publication by the curiously named Dick Whitington, a member of the Australian Services team in the mid-1940s, and a journalist:

> As he takes block, scratches with his boot-sprig those two lines in the popping crease that converge on the blockhole, takes a cursory, half self-conscious glance at the field-setting and finally tosses back the hair from his eyes, the whole atmosphere becomes charged with suspense. It is the same atmosphere when he deftly catches the ball from his captain and measures his run.
>
> The crowd expects some excitement and nine times out of ten is not disappointed. The unexpected is Miller's speciality. Maybe he has sent the ball skimming the sightboard like the buzz bombs skimmed the roofs of London. Perhaps the first ball has bumped past Bradman's eyebrow or disconnected Hutton's stump. Miller's cricket is high-spirited, and when allowed its natural beat, mostly uninhibited. It also bears the hallmark of high quality.

Serving with the RAAF in England, Miller was a Mosquito night-fighter pilot and crash landed one day near King's Lynn. The Mosquito was a write-off but Miller was indestructible. Within hours he was playing football for the airport team. Bothamesque, that. Aviation is almost a sub-theme to this chapter.

Miller was chosen for a daring raid on the airfields around Kiel Canal in 1945. The Mosquitoes were to drop tanks containing an inflammable jelly which would set fire to the hangars. Each plane carried a tank under either wing and each tank contained a Mills bomb to ignite on impact. Only one of Miller's tanks dropped when he pressed the release button over Kiel, and try as he might he could not shake the other one loose as he flew back to England across the North Sea. In serious danger of being blown to pieces, he landed at faster than normal speed, as instructed, and overshot the airstrip. The control officer could find no trace of the renegade tank. Miller was accused of causing unnecessary alarm until the tank was later discovered at the point of touchdown. It was in fragments, the fluid had spilled across the runway but the bomb had failed to explode!

Good fortune is another sub-plot, but then those who do not expose themselves to risk, either in a life-threatening or sporting context, do not invite that intangible factor into their world. *Homo sapiens* has the exclusive prerogative to take gratuitous risks because, alone in the animal kingdom, he is aware of his own existence. Zen Buddhism seeks an answer to the ultimate challenge of how to live in harmony with a world which is increasingly of our own making. Talent may be

God-given but cricket is man-made. An artificial set of circumstances which can dictate or be dictated to. Like war, you might say.

Compared to aerial warfare, cricket was tame to Miller, less a matter of life and death. He needed to inject some ginger into it. He lengthened his run and took Lord's by storm with 6–86 in a 1945 Victory 'Test' between England and the Australian Services side. No one, it seemed, had seen bowling so fast since Larwood's day. He crowned that first peacetime summer with a fabulous innings, again at Lord's, which made him a cricketing idol in London. His 185 for the Dominions XI was rated more highly than the two centuries posted by Wally Hammond for England in the same match. *Wisden* described it like this: 'Miller outshone everyone by dazzling hitting and, though travelling at the rate of 124 in 90 minutes, 185 in 165 minutes, he played absolutely faultless cricket.'

The Lord's pavilion came under heavy fire as seven of his 6s headed in that direction. One of them landed in the guttering of the pavilion roof. Two feet higher and Miller would have cleared the celebrated edifice, a feat achieved only by Albert Trott, a fellow Australian. Just as in Compton's case, Miller did not attach great importance to the tools of his trade. Cricket was less to do with bats, more to do with what went on in your head. Mr Whitington recalls:

'. . . the thrill seemed to have gone from hitting sixes straight down the line of flight over the bowler's head. Always an adventurer and a gambler, Miller had begun to hit more adventurously across the flight. The greater the risk, it seemed, the greater the fun . . . Miller had also developed a habit of picking up any old bat lying around and taking it out to the wicket, regardless of weight and regardless of ownership. A team-mate complained. Those cross-batted swings were making marks on the edges of his favourite blades.'

Winning at all costs did not figure in Miller's concept of sport. He preferred the Corinthian spirit expected at a time when the rewards for victory were not so high and cricket was more of an entertainment than a business. That was also true in W. G. Grace's day but few would pretend that the doctor did not have self-preservation and self-glorification at the top of his priority list. Miller was appalled at stories of W.G. replacing the bails when he was bowled, complaining of strong gusts of wind and batting on – or of scowling at the umpire when he was given out and insisting that the public had not come to watch the official give a silly decision but to watch *him* bat. W.G. was probably right, but should not the bowler have been taken into consideration? Miller's idea of cricket is exemplified by his soulmate from across the globe:

'I'm glad I never played with or against W. G. Grace. I prefer opponents like Denis Compton. Compton's record speaks for itself and his cricket's played in the spirit of the game that was originally intended. His greatest attribute is that he played even tense Test matches with the same calm that he wielded a Saturday afternoon bat. There was something about the way he sauntered out to the batting crease – casual perhaps, but with the ease that issues a direct challenge to opposing bowlers.'

After the war Compton became sport's first superstar. An Irish accountant, Bagenal Harvey, realized what potential earnings were at the command of a handsome cavalier who attracted two hundred fan letters a week – and this before the days of television. Harvey organized his new client's benefit in 1949 and was impressed, as he had a right to be, with the £12,000 it yielded. Further investigation by the accountant-turned-agent revealed that Compton was eminently suited to advertising endorsements and in considerable demand once his rates went up from £5 per photograph to nearer £100. By the beginning of the 1950s Brylcreem were paying him £1,500 a year to advertise their product, and the young lad from Hendon who had idolized Sir Jack Hobbs through his father's binoculars was a bigger name than his hero. The 'Brylcreem Boy' was the 1950s equivalent of the Shredded Wheat eater Ian Botham. Between them, no other cricketer attained showbiz status. At the time of writing they are still the only two larger-than-life personalities who have transcended the boundaries of cricket and made money in large quantities beyond the game. Compton was earning three times as much from his Brylcreem work as he was from Middlesex (even though, as one glance at his famous coiffure will tell you, he hardly ever used the unction). Nevertheless he was still working a full week at the age of seventy-three because the opportunities for lifetime investments were inversely proportional to the opportunities for a good time in post-war Britain – especially for a pin-up!

Botham is secure for life, despite or possibly because of his transgressions and a free spirit which failed to recognize bear-traps on or off the pitch. It is entirely in keeping that the man who saw nothing untoward about taking the long-handle to Lillee and Alderman should admit to having used drugs and should go for the throat of Henry Blofeld in full view of the nation's press when Botham discovered that the unsuspecting journalist had penned a less-than-sycophantic appraisal of his Caribbean captaincy for an Australian newspaper.

Those rushes of blood persuade Compton that he does not wish to be mentioned in the same breath as Botham. He must concede however that they share a kinship which sets them apart from any English cricketer in the last half a century.

Others have made an indelible mark, if not on quite the same scale. When it comes to adventurers with a touch of self-destruct, Brian Close is in a league of his own. He is, naturally, best remembered for his apparently suicidal handling of Hall and Griffith at Lord's in 1963. Taking several paces down the wicket to confront the world's fastest bowlers head-, or rather, chest-on was pure Compton. The rationale is pure Close.

'On the last day we kept losing time through rain and bad light. If we'd had time, we'd have won but they were taking four and a half minutes to bowl an over. I worked out we needed a run a minute to win and that's damned quick in a Test match! Each time we went off, Wes and Charlie had a chance to put their feet up then come straight back on when play resumed. We had to do something to upset them. What can you do to a fast bowler? Just before Wes bowled I picked up my bat and started walking just to plant myself between him and the stumps. If he was going to bowl straight, the only thing he could hit was me. There was no chance of an lbw because I was so far down. Wes was thrown off guard.'

To highlight Close's bravery, some would say folly, Cowdrey suffered a broken arm when a delivery from Hall climbed off the Lord's ridge. Hall and Griffith continued to lace their overs with bouncers, and with only nineteen minutes left, England needed 15 for victory. Close had reached 70, the highest score of the innings, when he decided more effrontery was required.

'That's when I walked down the wicket to Charlie. Most of the time you could put one hand in your pocket and play him with the other. Then he'd chuck one of his yorkers at you – or a bouncer – and they were about three times as quick. I reckoned I could lever him away over Kanhai at mid-wicket for 4. We could do the rest in ones and twos after that. If he tried a yorker it would be a full toss by the time I met it. I got my body in line and caught it with the under edge of my bat. I felt it brush my armpit before carrying twenty yards to [wicket-keeper] Deryck Murray. If it had hit my body we might have scrambled a bloody win.'

As it was, Cowdrey came back with his arm in plaster and England scrambled a draw. West Indies, arguably at their peak, went on to take the series 3–1. Close's superstructure was littered with bruises and the national newspapers revelled in the dressing-room photographs.

Close, loving every moment, made light of the punishment to his unprotected body. He still does.

'We only played with soft balls! I was never hit by a bouncer in my life. The only ones which hit me were the short-of-a-length ones which lifted. I took my hands and arms away and took the blows on the head or body. I accepted that. These days too many batsmen get hit on the hands and arms. That's bad batting.

'We played on uncovered wickets without helmets. I never had any fear because I was playing against fully grown men when I was eleven and professional footballers at Bradford Park Avenue when I was fourteen. That's when I learned that when you went on the field only one bloody thing mattered – winning.'

Close was never in favour with the selectors for very long. Astonishingly, his Test career began at the age of eighteen in 1949 and finished twenty-seven years later when he was recruited at the age of forty-five to counter the menace of Michael Holding and Andy Roberts. Beaten about the body again because he refused to wear a chest guard even in that theatre of fury, Close enjoyed exhibiting the scars of war. Bernie Thomas exhorted him to put his shirt back on: 'The lower-order batsmen were nervous enough without seeing the weals all over his chest. I told him to cover up or he'd frighten them to death. He thought it would have the opposite effect.'

Seventy was Close's top score in 22 Tests – hardly detectable in global terms – but his legacy to English cricket is enshrined in Yorkshire and Somerset folklore. His career went in three stages. At seventeen he was already 6 ft tall and reportedly bowling as fast as Fred Trueman, but his first voyage to Australia at nineteen set him back six years. He was out of his depth in the company of seasoned pros who were too intent, he says, on enjoying themselves after the deprivations of war to bother with an immature teenager. He conceived a hatred for the tour captain, Freddie Brown, and was hurt that his county colleague Len Hutton did not have time for him.

'By twenty I'd been through everything – success, failure, the lot. From doing the double in my first season to going to Australia as a kid and learning how cruel people could be, I learned what motivated them. Usually it was selfishness and jealousy.'

Stage Two was Close the Reluctant. Team-mates recall several occasions when he did not want to bat, could barely summon the enthusiasm to play at all. When he did he invariably carried an injury or an illness. The effect of that disappointment so early in his career was long-lasting and debilitating.

Stage Three came after Close was appointed Yorkshire captain in 1962. Then he was the 'Iron Man' ready and willing to take on all comers, including Hall and Griffith. His own assessment of cricket and its role in society ironically mirrors some of the personal crises that have hounded what might have been a much more productive Test career.

'I threw away my wicket so many times because my job was to make players play up to and beyond their abilities. That's the difference between Boycott and me. The game wasn't as important to him as his own success.

'We're a soft touch in this country. We've never lost a war but we don't start fighting until our backs are against the wall. Sport is a type of combat. It was developed for people to express their ability and competitive talent without killing each other. To take people to the edge. The problem is that if you don't have the killer instinct and you wait until your back's against the wall before hitting back, you can't win from that position – only draw. You've got to grab the initiative. That's been my message.

'I made it my business to understand the opposition. Over a drink and a chat I'd be getting to know their feelings and attitudes. The best time for psychology is out in the field as captain. Never let a batsman settle. Keep changing the bowling and the field placings so he's wondering: "Why has he done that?"

'We used to get wickets when we'd no right to get 'em. I captained my country seven times. We won six matches and drew one, then they dropped me because I knew how to put people together and get 'em performing. Take Bob Barber, for instance. I chose him because he was a damned good batsman who hardly bowled for Warwickshire. Against the West Indies I had him on before lunch and he got Sobers, the man who couldn't read leg-spinners. The second innings we got Sobers for a duck. I told John Snow to give him a short one because he was a compulsive hooker. Snowy let one go, Sobers went for it and got out. You've got to be imaginative in this game. Take gambles. Hoodwink people.

'Johnny Wardle was the best at that. He was as cute as a box of monkeys. Told me to make it as a first-class cricketer you had to have bottle and brain. When Boycott took over the Yorkshire captaincy from me they went downhill fast. Don Wilson couldn't bowl any more. Boycott didn't understand how to get the best out of people. Don was a good flighter of the ball but didn't turn it much. I'd made the opposition think he was turning it by switching him around the wicket. Or conversely on a responsive wicket, we'd kid them Don wasn't doing much then get him to turn one and catch 'em off guard.'

The relationship between Close and Ray Illingworth goes back to teenage years but Close feels that Illy would have been even more successful had he adopted a more daredevil approach.

'Illy would let things happen on their own by keeping things tight. He wouldn't experiment much. I couldn't play games like that. I wanted to go out and make it happen. To every situation there's an answer and you have to find it. If you don't, the game dictates to you. Many times I put Ray on to bowl when he didn't fancy it. He'd be happy to get through 20-odd overs and take 1–24. I wouldn't allow that. I wanted 20 overs and 4–40. Something to turn the match. I didn't lose many.'

For all his derring-do and bravado, Close is a warm-hearted, somewhat bashful personality underneath. A complex one, full of contradictions. Bernie Thomas again:

'Like Tony Greig, Brian wouldn't show fear or anxiety. It didn't mean he didn't feel any. People have different interpretations of pain and discomfort. Brian would take a fearful blow on the head or the leg without acknowledging it even though he might be bleeding. Yet the same man in a situation he wasn't familiar with – with a cold or an infection – was a kitten. It seems to be a trait with Yorkshiremen. Chris Old was always fretting about an ache or a sniffle. John Hampshire was terrified at the sight of blood.'

Life itself was and is an adventure to 'Lord' Ted Dexter. He sped up and down Britain's motorways on a Harley Davidson conducting his search for fast bowlers to frighten the West Indies (he wasted a lot of fuel), and once piloted himself and his family to Australia in his own light aeroplane to report on an MCC tour. His cricket was straight out of the Compton/Botham school of attacking batsmanship although Dexter adhered much more closely to the textbook when it came to technique. Curiously he also scored 70 against the might of Hall and Griffith in that 1963 Test at Lord's, but whereas Close's innings was built on defiance and courage, Dexter's effort in the England first innings was designed to prove that pacemen were just as likely to capitulate under heavy bombardment as spin bowlers. It was a glorious and audacious assault although a mere cameo instead of a full-length feature. Such was Dexter.

I can remember now how the excitement in our school cricket pavilion reached fever pitch as we listened to the BBC radio broadcast. How anyone could react at all to Wes Hall's missiles let alone bludgeon them to the long-off and extra-cover boundaries was beyond us. From what we could gather Dexter was not waiting for the bad ball but employing scattergun tactics, lashing everything in sight. As invigorating as it was, we suspected it could not last and it did not. Having completed three score and ten, Dexter was trapped leg before by Sobers. His knock lasted 81 minutes.

'I decided that day after two wickets down to take the battle to them or we'd have been rolled over. I always felt good against pacemen so I gave it everything I'd got. It wasn't throwing caution to the wind, it was more a case of forcing the bowlers to think less about getting you out and more about how to avoid being hit for another 4. I saw Hall and Griffith off, which was the first part of the mission completed.

'When I was out there, one man against eleven, it was daunting but I'd given Wes a fair hammering in the West Indies a few years earlier and knew if I hung around for half an hour things would change. It's amazing how they always do. The magic of cricket is to be able to tilt the game gradually in your favour so that eventually you have eleven men at your beck and call. That's a real high, a marvellous feeling of power and the absolute quintessence of the game at the top level. There's no finer feeling in sport.'

Apart from graduating at Cambridge and captaining the university before bursting on to the scene as a lively medium-pacer with 5–8 for the Gentlemen v. Players in 1957, Dexter also became a prodigious golfer. He makes an interesting analogy between the two sports in which the still-ball game (perhaps surprisingly) emerges as the more pressurized.

'The pressure you feel at the start of an innings when the ball's flying past your ears can seem impossible to bear but it wears away and never comes back. In contrast it increases in golf, especially when you've been in the lead. You're playing yourself, not reacting naturally to the moving ball. Often I've stood over a shot with the club shaking in my hands wondering if I'll manage to make contact with the ball. I've never felt like that with a cricket bat in my hands.'

The comfort he felt when facing the quicks was enhanced once chest protectors were introduced, although like any true adventurer, he is unimpressed by helmets.

'We didn't realize how wonderful it could be until we got chest protectors. You could let the ball hit your body and you didn't feel a thing. It was bloody marvellous. Neil Adcock was one of the meanest bowlers. He really used to make the ball fly at you. But I learned to take a few on the body and when Neil followed through to finish about three yards from the batsman's nose it was nice to smile at him untroubled while he tried to fix you with that glare of his. We had no head protectors until Mike Brearley appeared with his temple guards. We didn't get many injuries because unlike the batsmen of today we watched the ball all the way. Against those chaps you had to.'

For all his imperious skills and spellbinding gift of commanding the stage, Dexter was a little slow to make his mark as a Test batsman and too frequently got himself out with a careless shot while apparently on his way to a big score. How perverse that his two biggest Test innings – 180 and 174 – were protracted defensive affairs which saved rather than won matches against Australia. When he was given his head, he could produce the sort of innings which might win a limited-over contest but was too rapid for a Test match. We only have to cast our minds back to Old Trafford 1961 for a perfect example of that, although Dexter could hardly be blamed for a stirring innings which should have inspired England to victory, not precipitated a collapse. Peter May was captain in what has become known as Richie Benaud's Test:

'Dexter let us down. We should have been playing for a draw so we could go to the Oval all square at one each. After Ted's innings we were thinking we might have a chance of winning after all.'

His crime had been to batter 76 runs off the Australian attack in the fourth innings of a fluctuating game. England seemed to be home and dry until Alan Davidson and Graham McKenzie, on a wicket that was starting to turn, put on 99 for the last wicket of Australia's second innings. Brian Close had been recalled after the almost mandatory two-year absence:

'Peter May was a great batsman but his thoughts on cricket sometimes let him down. I was watching from the balcony. Geoff Pullar made a good start, then Ted played brilliantly to put us well on the way. We "won" that game twice and ended up losing it because of pathetic leadership. In the dressing-room we felt we had a great chance. We needed a plan, but no one said anything. I saw Raman Subba Row playing for himself as sheet anchor and Dexter carving them to ribbons. Suddenly Benaud decided to go around the wicket to try to stop England winning. He thought that bowling into the rough Fred Trueman had made outside leg-stump would slow us down and give them the draw they were desperate for. Didn't anybody know? Dexter got out almost the first ball Richie bowled. It spun out of the rough and he was taken behind the wicket. I'm talking to Peter May and begging him not to put two left-handers together – me and Subba

Row. So he goes in himself and gets bowled around his legs trying to sweep Benaud's second ball. So I'm in. Two left-handers. Subba Row never made one effort to play a positive shot against "Slasher" Mackay, the bloke we should have been going after, so I felt I had to take the law into my own hands. Richie pitched one up and I drove him for 6. Soon afterwards I connected just about perfectly aiming Richie over square-leg, but Norman O'Neill dived full length and caught it with two hands. They blew me out after that. We threw wickets away not knowing whether we were going for a win or a draw and I was crucified.'

May's version continues:

'Dear old Closey. I wasn't very good getting out so quickly, but he played a pretty stupid innings as is his wont. Fancy trying to sweep the thing out of the ground in those circumstances. This was Richie's fourth tour of England and that's the only performance of his anyone remembers. He never got many wickets in England.'

The captain was playing his last series. Recurring ill-health and business distractions brought to an end his 41–Test reign. Only ten of them, including Old Trafford, were lost. Let us go back to the innocent villain of that controversial last day, Dexter himself. There was more to the story than either May or Close knew or was letting on:

'The captain moved me up the order to No. 3 because he said he couldn't be certain of my attitude in a tight corner. I was more of an impulsive stroke-maker. Davidson and Mackay were no problem. We looked to have the match sewn up. Then when we scored only 80-odd runs between lunch and tea, the chairman of selectors, Gubby Allen, who'd apparently had one of those lunches which starts at one o'clock and goes through to the tea interval, came ranting and raving into the dressing-room demanding to know what the hell Barrington was doing batting so slowly. To rave on like that was disgraceful. It undermined morale. The next thing we lost 5 wickets for 20 runs and victory was turned into defeat. Benaud did well to keep pitching into the rough but he was lucky. It got into the players' minds. We fell apart quite needlessly.'

Australia won by 54 runs, Benaud taking 5–12 in 25 balls, to take a 2–1 lead. The Oval Test was drawn so the Ashes stayed with Australia.

Dexter had a love-indifference relationship with cricket. Occasionally criticized for practising his tee shot when his mind should have been on the match, he was not completely convinced that cricket was a worthy métier for a highly educated and gifted dilettante.

'I got into it by finding I could do it successfully at a certain level and

ENGLAND v AUSTRALIA
Old Trafford 1961

AUSTRALIA

Lawry lbw b Statham	74—c Trueman b Allen	102
Simpson c Murray b Statham	4—c Murray b Flavell	51
Harvey c Subba Row b Statham	19—c Murray b Dexter	35
O'Neill hit wkt b Trueman	11—c Murray b Statham	67
Binge b Flavell	15—c Murray b Dexter	23
Booth c Close b Statham	46—lbw b Dexter	9
Mackay c Murray b Statham	11—c Close b Allen	18
Davidson c Barrington b Dexter	0—not out	77
Benaud b Dexter	2—lbw b Allen	1
Grout c Murray b Dexter	2—c Statham b Allen	0
McKenzie not out	1—b Flavell	32
Extras	5—Extras	17
	190	**432**

Bowling: *First Innings*—Simpson 4–23; Davidson 3–70.
Second Innings—Benaud 32–11–70–6

ENGLAND

Pullar b Davidson	63—c O'Neill b Davidson	26
Subba Row c Simpson b Davidson	2—b Benaud	49
Dexter c Davidson b McKenzie	16—c Grout b Benaud	76
May c Simpson b Davidson	95—b Benaud	0
Close lbw McKenzie	33—c O'Neill b Benaud	8
Barrington c O'Neill b Simpson	78—lbw b Mackay	5
Murray c Grout b Mackay	24—c Simpson b Benaud	4
Allen c Booth b Simpson	42—c Simpson b Benaud	10
Trueman c Harvey b Simpson	3—c Benaud b Simpson	8
Statham c Mackay b Simpson	4—b Davidson	8
Flavell not out	0—not out	0
Extras	7—Extras	7
	367	**201**

Bowling: *First Innings*—Statham 5–53; Dexter 3–16.
Second Innings—Allen 4–58; Dexter 3–61

wanting to know whether I could master it at the highest level. Once I discovered I could, cricket became a great turn-on. Then I began to wonder what I was doing in this business. I remember walking out on a Thursday in Kanpur in 90-degree heat for a day in the field, thinking there must be something more to life than this. Was this what I had studied to be?

'As captain when none of the things we tried in the field came off I used to think, "What the hell? – I can't do much about this." That's when my mind started to wander and I'd give the impression of being detached.'

In 1965 Dexter resigned as captain of Sussex after breaking a leg. To all intents and purposes his career seemed to be over. Three years later he deemed it *à propos* to make a comeback, scoring 203 in his first innings, and his form persuaded the selectors to pick him for the last two Tests against Australia. He did not disappoint them:

'When I broke my leg I stopped to think about my future in the game. I'd played against every country, done the circuit, captained against practically everyone. What was I going to do? The whole circuit again? Today, with the rewards, you might be inclined to say "yes". At the time there was no real money to be earned. I thought it was about time I did a *real* job and started making a reasonable living to support my family. Then there came a time when I regretted giving up. My business wasn't terribly enjoyable and I wasn't that good at it. Why do it when I could be running about on the international cricket field enjoying myself and doing a much better job? That period passed. Now I can sit back and enjoy the changing face of a sport which has dominated my life.'

Dominated, yes, but not dictated. Dexter would be the last person to close the door on other avenues of discovery. He obviously respects the right of other individuals not to treat cricket as a matter of life and death, otherwise as chairman of selectors he would surely not have sanctioned Botham's special leave of absence as the England party set off for New Zealand and the World Cup in Australia at the end of 1991, allowing him to continue in pantomime and join the squad at a later date. Ted's predecessor, Peter May, was horrified.

'No one's bigger than the game. I wouldn't have let Botham in the party. You can't say, "I'm sorry, I'm at Bournemouth in a panto, I'll miss the start of the trip." I told Micky Stewart he'd picked hassle. He said, "What do you mean?" I said, "I can't say it in plainer English." It was no good talking to Ted because Gooch and Micky pick the team.'

May, along with many others, underestimated Beefy's influence on

the England team. Even Dermot Reeve, an heir apparent to his throne
and doubtful admirer, reported that Botham had been an enormous
help during the World Cup, and had shown him how to swing the ball
more than ever before. And I shudder to imagine May's reactions
when the headline 'Pantomime Star Flattens Aussies' accompanied
Botham's four-wicket demolition and bruising half-century.

England's new hard-line regime could be accused of betraying
double standards by jettisoning David Gower after his fly-past at
Brisbane. Gower would have done his own cause a power of good if he
had committed himself more fully to Gooch's Australian tour of
1990–91 which was an abysmal failure; his prank might then have
been accepted in the spirit in which it was undertaken and Dexter, an
aviator himself, would have been the first to applaud it. As it was,
Gower probably piloted himself off the radar screen and into Test
match oblivion. Gower's *raison d'être* is dealt with in another chapter.

Botham apart, the most swashbuckling player of the modern era
was his old Somerset team-mate Viv Richards, although they were
poles apart temperamentally. Viv's talent was unique – a cocktail of
power, beauty and improvisation – but, except for the early days, he
was not the carefree cavalier he seemed. Nothing like as carefree as Sir
Gary Sobers, whose laid-back approach to both captaincy and batting
exasperated Clive Lloyd. Richards is a complex personality, deeply
conscious of his roots and his debt to the impoverished society which
spawned him. He is also a loner. Trevor McDonald in his authorized
biography put it this way:

> . . . his tendency still, in moments of the most agonizing pressure, to fly
> off the handle will be a deciding factor about how long he leads the
> West Indies. Another problem might be his pride. His team-mates talk
> about his aristocratic air; the manner of his walk to the wicket; the way
> he plays the game, hardly ever tailoring his natural aggression to
> conditions in which lesser men would plod around and play with the
> utmost care and defence. But knowing you are probably the best
> batsman alive puts enormous strain on a player.

The 1976 series between West Indies and England during the hottest,
driest summer then on record brought Richards into conflict with
another magnetic personality, Tony Greig. They were light years apart
in ability, as Greig would be quick to concede. Nevertheless when it
came to gung-ho leadership, the South African – son of a Scots father –
was in a class of his own. Misguided sometimes, over-ebullient
frequently but almost impossible to demoralize. That has not been
true of Viv.

Richards's smouldering resentment of the role the black man had been constrained to play since being transported to the Caribbean colonies to work on the plantations was stoked into life when Greig made his unfortunate 'grovel' remark before Lloyd's men touched down at Gatwick. Greig had already enjoyed success in the West Indies as a player under Mike Denness and, more importantly, had stopped the rot after taking over the captaincy from Denness in the summer of 1975 when Lillee and Thomson threatened to run amok. So he was on something of a 'high' when he uttered his over-optimistic inanity. Viv and Clive say they were shocked and angered by it, but I believe the issue has been hyped out of proportion. International sportsmen are accustomed to threats, challenges and pseudo insults, usually issued through and embellished by the newspapers. This was the verbal equivalent of Marvin Hagler and Sugar Ray Leonard standing toe-to-toe and nose-to-nose before the big fight; pre-match baloney which did wonders for ticket sales and TV viewing figures – of which Greig was soon to become acutely aware.

At any rate, Richards was energized. We had seen nothing of him as a Test batsman on English shores. He had cut his teeth on the West Indies tour of India, completing his maiden Test century (192) at New Delhi before excelling in the home series with centuries in the first three Tests. Greig did not have the artillery with which to enforce his battle cry against a West Indian side reaching the height of its powers. Richards began the summer with 232 dashing runs at Trent Bridge and wrapped it up with 291 in the final Test at the Oval where West Indies won the rubber 3–0. Viv averaged 118 in the series, entertaining us with outrageous stroke-play including his favourite flick through mid-wicket.

Throughout his career he was especially severe on Bob Willis. Stepping outside leg-stump to strike him through extra-cover was not so much punishing one of the world's leading wicket-takers as treating him with disdain. Willis bears no grudges.

'He used to hit grooved balls for 6 or 4. He hit me for 24 in an over at Old Trafford. There's a lot of psyching going on when you bowl to them. After hitting you for 4 he takes the p—— by over-accentuating his defensive block when he could just as easily have dispatched that one over to the boundary as well. Notice the way when he comes in to bat he always waits until the outgoing batsman is well out of sight. I've seen him in the Caribbean delay his entrance until the drinks interval was over. He wasn't going to walk out unheralded while everyone was distracted by a bloody drinks trolley!'

Sobers played a more classical game. Richards, on the face of it, got away with murder. In truth both had the quickness of eye and the reflexes to react to almost any delivery in whichever way they chose. After nervous beginnings during which his skipper showed limitless faith in him, Richards drew strength and confidence from his own supremacy. A touch of arrogance is permissible, even desirable in the circumstances. One or two county bowlers who shall remain nameless have been made to feel shatteringly humble in the presence of the great man. He would apparently talk them into submission with comments like, 'Shit ball, man!' before driving them back over their heads. Remarks such as that were more likely to have been a statement of self-gratification than an outpouring of personal abuse, for cricket and winning have always meant more to him than hitting a ball across a field. We must remember that there is another dimension to the game in the Caribbean. Listen to Lester Bird, the former prime minister of Antigua:

'The country needed a focal point, a touchstone which could form the basis of communal unity in a common cause. Richards represented that touchstone: he was the embodiment of an opportunity for a whole nation to be galvanized for a single purpose. The common cause, that single purpose, became Viv Richards's success on the international cricket stage . . . . He personified what we perceived ourselves to be; young, dynamic and talented but yet unrecognized in the world.'

Imagine the pride which burned in the breasts of native islanders as Viv scored a century against England when the first-ever Test match was staged in his home town of St Johns, Antigua in 1981!

Towards the end of his career in the English summer of 1991, Viv at thirty-nine years of age was noticeably more circumspect as a batsman. Commentators pointed out that he was playing straight down the line rather more than usual. Was he mellowing in his dotage?

'I think I've mellowed ever since I started playing Test cricket. For some reason I've accumulated more than 8,000 runs in my own particular way. You have to have your own style. People like the Michael Jordans of this world don't do the things that the normal individual does. That's why he is who he is. That's why Nike offer him such a big contract. Viv Richards likes to do things differently too. Things that other people don't know about. Hitting across the line of the ball has made me successful for a number of years. I wouldn't preach this to any youngster because he may not be able to go out there and do it. All I would say is that if the game comes more easily doing it your way, don't let anyone put you off.'

That was Tony Greig's philosophy too. Since he discovered as a twelve-year-old that he was epileptic, life – and sport in particular – took on a different perspective. It did not take him long to realize that obeying doctor's orders would imprison a free spirit. How could an adventurous, energetic young boy growing up in South Africa cut cycling, swimming and rock-climbing out of his schedule? Greig decided to risk it and was fortunate to get away with his imprudence. His Grand Mal seizures were quickly under control thanks to a daily dose of tablets to which all epileptics are tied. The malfunction is incurable but controllable to the extent that Greig (at the time of writing) had not suffered an attack for eighteen years. Neither has he ever offered it as an excuse. Indeed when he 'flaked out' at the Wanderers Ground in Johannesburg in 1970 the collapse was attributed to heat exhaustion and the press kept the truth to themselves. 'I collapsed soon after getting up that morning and the doctor advised me not to play. It was to be my debut for Eastern Province so I stubbornly insisted I was fit to play. I remember taking two slip catches off Peter Pollock before throwing back my head, spinning around and collapsing in a heap.'

That man Henry Blofeld erroneously suggested that the pills Greig takes were responsible for his decision to join World Series Cricket. Any epileptic – and there are more of them than people think – will tell you that the remark is too absurd to deserve an answer. Says Greig:

'Epilepsy probably did me a lot of good. I think getting over a few serious hurdles makes you a better equipped person. My father's an alcoholic but he's got that licked and he's a stronger individual now. Compared to your health, other worries in life can seem not as important as you make them out to be. I believed in playing cricket the way I've lived my life. There has to be a bit of danger. I love racing motor cars. Holidays without monkey ropes and jet-skis aren't really holidays. I was brought up in an environment where challenge was the key word. When we went away we'd go hunting wild boar or guinea fowl, and it was like being on the front at Gallipoli. You didn't want to be the bloke who buggered it up!'

Dennis Amiss, one of Greig's WSC colleagues, and now an England selector, relates a hair-raising experience when he (Greig) took the wheel of a hire car in New Zealand and insisted on accelerating around the mountains as though he were at Brands Hatch.

'He made Derek Underwood, me and this New Zealand guy who was organizing the trip put on our cricket helmets before he shot off like a maniac. Greigy kept turning round and asking, "Everything okay in the back?" and we were shouting, "For Christ's sake slow down!" Then we came to a mountain pass and it was starting to drizzle. Greig was going as fast as he could. Suddenly we saw a car coming the other way. He braked and we went into a skid. Below us was a sheer drop of about 300 feet. Miraculously there was a mound of earth by the roadside and we smashed into it. The poor guy in the passenger seat was now facing Greigy because he'd been gripping the seat so tightly it came off its ratchets! Our driver thought it was great fun. He's got a thousand lives, not nine. He could have wiped out a quarter of the team. I never drove with him again.'

That same disregard for hazard characterized his approach to cricket. Although he was first and foremost a winner, there was nothing Greig relished more than a struggle against adversity. He found plenty of that in Australia in 1974–75 when Lillee and Thomson laid waste to Denness's retreating troops. As early as the first Test in Brisbane, Greig was taking the pacemen on at their own game, declining to back off an inch. It was more than a man with a bat facing men with a ball, it was a clash of willpowers. In the first phase of the battle, Greig was a clear winner. He managed to rattle Lillee, something no other member of the team had the temerity to attempt.

'I wasn't afraid to have a go at someone if I thought that by upsetting them I could throw them off key. That's fair game. It's only a question then of where you draw the line and how antagonistic you want to be. I concentrated on Lillee at Brisbane. Wound him up a treat. The result was that he was more intent on killing me than getting me out, and that was in my best interest. I had him psychologically. The shorter he pitched it, the easier it was for me to cut him away for 4. He got more and more exhausted with the effort of trying to bang it in short. I told him he wasn't bowling fast enough. If he hadn't allowed himself to be psyched out of it he'd probably have got me out. As it was he completely lost his cool, swearing and cursing like a trooper while I helped myself to a hundred.'

Quintessential Greig, showing the qualities which marked him as a natural leader and, paradoxically, persuaded an external force to seduce him away from the top job in the country just when he was most needed. Amiss was inspired by that century, though it was a desperately unhappy tour for him:

'Greig first took them on when we were bowling. He fired a bouncer at Lillee who finished in a heap after gloving it to Alan Knott. The tables are turned when we batted. Greig goes in at six and Lillee's aching for his revenge. He shouts: "After what you did to me I'm going to kill you, you —— ——!" Greig just answers back with his silly high-pitched laugh. Unbelievable. Dennis gets even more worked up then. It was magnificent to see but we're not all Greigs. I was at the other end thinking, "Bloody hell, he's going to take it out on me!"

'In the meantime my partner stands there, cool as you like, ducking inside bouncers. Then he hits one through the covers calling to Lillee: "That's four, take that!" The bowler grabs the ball, mumbling as he walks past me something about knocking his head off. The next one goes for four as well and there's Greig doing the umpire's signal shouting: "There you go, four more." Lillee was absolutely seething. I knew we were in for a hell of a tour.'

Similarly when Holding was bowling out of his skin at the Oval in 1976, Amiss felt a chill go up his spine upon the arrival at the crease of Mr Grovel himself. The rubber was already safely in the West Indies' hands but Amiss had been weathering the cyclone.

'We'd lost a few wickets but it was fairly calm and we looked as if we might make a big score. Greig had other ideas. He said, "Right, I'm going to stir them up now. I'll get 'em going, you see." That's what he had to do to motivate himself. I said, "Don't you dare. It's nice and peaceful out here!" He laughed. Holding bowled him leg-stump before he could get his bat down. In a way I was glad he didn't hang around to cause trouble. He just had to be confrontational whereas some of us wanted a quiet time – a village green atmosphere.' There is an odd sequel to this which indicates that Greig was not always as sure of himself as he appeared. At one moment in the 1976 series, it needed Alan Knott's persuasive powers to prevent his throwing in the towel. He was human after all.

'The older players used to tell me to cool it but I was young and full of mischief. At the end I'd always have a drink with the bloke I'd been having a go at. Dennis Amiss couldn't understand that. Lillee terrorized the life out of him then offered to get him a beer. That's the way I was brought up in South Africa. We played a lot of rugby union which fosters that kind of camaraderie. You knock hell out of each other for eighty minutes, crash tackling and punching, but you're happy together with a beer at the end.'

Boredom was and is Greig's greatest enemy, not only because he is hyperactive but because it is a well-known trigger for epilepsy. If he was trapped in the dressing-room for long periods he would sleep. If he was making a transworld flight he would often break the journey, take a couple of sleeping tablets and check into a hotel for the night before resuming the flight next morning.

'It's not negotiable. As soon as I get any hint of dizziness I make sure I sleep. I did in the Centenary Test. It was no problem to me to sleep when I was next in – without tablets. When I walked out to bat, though, I'd have as much adrenalin as the next man. After that it's a question of how good you are at controlling it. The Boycotts and Lawrys of this world are masters at controlling adrenalin over long periods, patient players who were hungry in a different way. I got more fun out of having a go and smashing someone out of the attack.'

Apart from his epic century in Calcutta when flu and heat combined to rob him of his energy, Greig's other exceptional turn was in Trinidad in 1973–74 when England needed victory to square the series at 1–1. Boycott's innings of 99 and 112 were the cornerstones but it was Greig the bowler who won the game in the most unexpected fashion. Throughout the series he had been purveying his usual seamers on flat wickets, to no avail. Not to put too fine a point on it, Lloyd and company were treating it as cannon fodder. Greig, for the first time in his career, was 'spooked'. Reports Dennis Amiss:

'Greig had nightmares about Clive plonking his leg down the wicket to a straight ball and decapitating him. "I can't bowl," he said, "he'll kill me." Greigy had gone. He started bowling little off-cutters in self-defence. They got better and better.'

He can say that again. Greig took 8–86 in the West Indies' first innings and 5–70 in the second. They were easily the best bowling figures he had – and from such modest beginnings.

At the end of the Indian tour of 1976–77 Greig basked in the welcome glory of having led England to an impressive 3–1 victory over Bishen Bedi's men and become the first Englishman to score 3,000 Test runs and take 100 wickets. The sky seemed to be the limit as he headed for the Melbourne Centenary Test. It was, but not with England. However much they pilloried him for his defection, Greig had been made an offer by Kerry Packer which would secure his future and present him with fresh challenges. Being the adventurer he is, how could he refuse?

TWO

The Enigma

'The mass of men lead lives of quiet desperation.'
HENRY DAVID THOREAU

In the sparkling sunlight of Australia and the Caribbean, batsmen who are keen of eye and steady of nerve can identify the rotation of the spinning ball as it loops towards them. No urgency in that case to read it leaving the hand nor any pressure to play it off the pitch, a hazardous occupation even on wickets offering only moderate assistance to the bowler. For all that, Wally Hammond was most at home with the last of the three options, as indeed in more recent years was John Edrich. Such eleventh-hour adjustments demand the sharpest of reflexes and carry maximum risk.

According to Colin Cowdrey, Hammond could not be bothered watching the ball leave the hand. 'He'd play it the moment it hit the ground which is quite staggering. I wanted it earlier than that because on an overcast day you had to work bloody hard to keep it out of your stumps. Wally didn't mind. Sir Don was the same. Their judgement was acute.'

Reading the spin in mid-air is a profound joy to those batsmen equipped to do it. When Sonny Ramadhin was bowling it seemed to be the only hope, although in English conditions and because of the speed at which he bowled, it was often a forlorn hope.

As a purveyor of sorcery across the cricketing globe Ramadhin was unique. For seven hard-working years in the 1950s he bemused the world's best batsmen and repeatedly defied all attempts to unravel his mysteries. That fact is doubly remarkable when you consider how many overs he was called upon to bowl. Ramadhin says Keith Miller, Len Hutton and Ken Barrington came closest to finding the antidote. Miller because he stepped down the wicket and hit across the line; Hutton because he was so painstaking; and Barrington because he watched the ball spinning in the air. 'You have to be very sharp to do that,' says Sonny.

It all changed on a Monday and Tuesday in June 1957 at Edgbaston.

Peter May, in partnership with Colin Cowdrey, applied his mind to the task with such diligence and determination that the little Trinidadian with the buttoned-down sleeves was effectively finished as a Test match bowler. Seldom has the initiative been wrested back so suddenly and with such finality. It was one of my earliest memories; Peter May became a childhood hero. In a household which was football orientated, cricket won my allegiance. Fast bowlers get tired and need a rest but Ramadhin just kept on bowling. Every ball was loaded with dynamite. How did May and Cowdrey emerge so victorious when disaster was only one little slip away?

Life had dealt Ramadhin an unimpressive hand among the wooden huts of San Fernando where he grew up as an orphan, friendless and nameless until someone christened him 'Sonny'. *Wisden* conferred on him the initials K.T. because he had none of his own. Life was cruel to him again in 1990 when Bass along with other breweries was forced by the Monopolies Commission to sell a number of its pubs to the highest bidders and Ramadhin, the teetotal landlord of The White Lion at Delph near Oldham, was forced out. He and his wife Sharon, a local girl, lost their livelihood and the roof over their heads. Council accommodation wasn't easy to come by but happily they found it.

Sonny could be excused for harbouring the odd grudge, but there is not an ounce of resentment in him. When I met him during his last few days in the pub – ironically just before Christmas – I was taken by his modesty. A more self-effacing individual you could hardly imagine. How, I wondered, could such a mild-mannered fellow, standing a mere 5 ft 4 in in his stockinged feet, have tormented the likes of Lindsay Hassett, Denis Compton, Neil Harvey, Cyril Washbrook, Tom Graveney and Arthur Morris to name only a few? It isn't sufficient to be a good bowler or even an exceptional one in that company. A spinner must have unshakeable belief in his ability or he is a dead man.

In his pomp, Ramadhin was lethal. The West Indies, for whom spin bowling became anathema in the 1970s and 1980s, relied almost exclusively on the Ramadhin/Valentine combination once they had taken the very bold step of selecting the two nineteen-years-olds to tour England in 1950. John Goddard, the West Indies captain, would have taken little persuading to open the bowling with them. The pair would tweak away all day – Valentine, the left-armer, a master of flight and capable of prodigious turn; Ramadhin the enigma, with his unfathomable mixture of leg- and off-spin which had batsmen groping in permanent penumbra. Guessing, always guessing, no matter whether they had been at the crease for ten minutes or two hours. The problem was that the leg-break, like the off-break, was delivered with finger spin. That was unheard of.

West Indies cricket at that time was entering a purple period, albeit brief. Goddard had led them to a 1–0 series victory on their first-ever trip to India, with Everton Weekes blasting centuries all around the subcontinent. The other two-thirds of the three Ws, Frank Worrell and Clyde Walcott, had just begun to show their mettle too, while Jeff Stollmeyer and Allan Rae had emerged as the best opening partnership in the history of Caribbean cricket. The England bowlers knew they were in for a tough summer.

The weakness in the touring party looked for all the world to lie in the bowling department. Hines Johnson, at forty, could not sensibly be expected to create much havoc in the autumn of his career. Goddard and the selectors had to gamble. The result was electrifying. Alf Valentine, a 6 ft machinist from Speightstown, Jamaica, gained selection on the strength of taking 2–151 in a series between his home island and Trinidad. If the credentials did not scream at you, the potential did. Ramadhin's pedigree was even sketchier. Before catching the boat to England his only experience of first-class cricket was two trial games for Trinidad under the watchful gaze of Stollmeyer, the captain. He liked what he saw. The teenager whose reputation for wizardry had spread through Trinidad like bushfire was, he thought, ready to be unleashed on Hutton and Co. What a sea change.

'I never knew I could get anywhere near the West Indies team. Until the trials I had only played village cricket. A chap called Skinner who worked for Trinidad Leaseholds Ltd (Texaco these days) gave me a job as groundsman when I left school. That meant I cut the grass and made the wickets just so that I could play. Word got around that I was taking six, seven or eight wickets every week. That's when they sent for me at Port of Spain. Val and I started together there.'

From the age of four Sonny was brought up by an uncle after his father died of diabetes. Mr Ramadhin senior had, by all accounts, played a bit of cricket himself. It was certainly in his son's blood although the business of batting held no attraction for him. Spin bowling was a passion.

'It came naturally. As a youngster I played on dirt. A sort of red clay which was rolled. You only had to turn your arm over and the ball spun square. Later on we played on coir matting. It's like jute but thicker and knitted. I learned to bowl on that before I came to England. They played Tests on jute. You couldn't bowl a side out on it.'

Valentine was first to settle into his rhythm when the tour began, taking 8–104 on a helpful wicket at Old Trafford. Ramadhin opened his career with a disappointing 2–90. Godfrey Evans played the turning ball well, his experience of keeping wicket to Doug Wright at Kent enabling him to feel more at ease with Ramadhin's brisk, skidding style. Godfrey says he picked the spin in flight and came to the conclusion that the one thrown a little higher was usually the leg-break. His judgement served him well on his way to his maiden first-class century in a match-winning stand of 161 with Trevor Bailey.

England duly won that first Test with something to spare. It was to be their last success. The performances of 'Ram and Val' entranced the nation and the world of cricket. As C.L.R. James, the West Indian writer, points out, great slow bowlers would normally take several years to mature. When Bill O'Reilly and Clarry Grimmett dominated the English batting in 1934, O'Reilly was twenty-nine and Grimmett forty-two. Somehow the two West Indians had the world at their mercy as they celebrated their twentieth birthdays.

The English counties were mesmerized by Ramadhin who collected 135 wickets at 14.88 runs each on the tour. No one could distinguish the leg-break from his standard delivery, the off-break, because each was conjured from identical arm actions and approaches to the wicket. Remarkably for someone so young, Ramadhin had established a psychological superiority over his opponents that, arguably, no spin bowler has achieved since. Phil Tufnell may yet outstrip him.

Jim Laker 'freaked' the Australians in 1956 both at Old Trafford and with his earlier 10-wicket haul for Surrey at the Oval, but his success was achieved by supreme control of line, length and flight rather than mystery; collective hysteria and a drying Manchester wicket had something to do with it as well.

The Pakistani wrist-spinner Abdul Qadir was indecipherable to most county batsmen when he first appeared in 1982 but, having helped to inspire his country's second victory over England with six wickets at Lord's, he finished the Test series with only ten altogether. Five years later he wrote his name into the history books with 9–56 as Pakistan beat England by an innings in Lahore. His efforts were overshadowed by the stand-up row between Mike Gatting and Shakoor Rana, the Pakistani umpire, in a series which turned very sour. Gatting, an outstanding player of spin, still regards those figures of Qadir's as suspect but acknowledges that he was a fine bowler:

'I watch the ball out of the hand and the only time you have a problem reading it is with someone like Qadir who bowls leggies with a top-spinner and googly thrown in. I didn't find him mysterious. You had to concentrate on every ball. As long as you did, the clues were always there.'

There was a period in the early fifties when every Indian schoolboy wanted to bowl like Subash Gupte. Having been discarded as a potentially expensive luxury, the leg-spinner from Bombay more than held his own against the three Ws in 1952. Some achievement, although hard, bouncy wickets should certainly have been his cup of Darjeeling. To suggest that he mastered the West Indies batsmen would be inaccurate, but they did not quite master him. Gupte flighted and spun the ball so devilishly that he came home with 27 Test wickets to his name. Ivan Madray, the West Indian leg-spinner who was inspired by Gupte although not to the same heights, was impressed with the way he kept his head while all around were losing theirs.

'On a number of occasions when he was hit, he would stroll back slowly, thoughtfully, to his bowling mark, as if nothing had happened and when you thought he was giving you the leg-break again, he would bowl his beautifully disguised googly or he would toss it up or shift it. He would try everything in one over, a different ball each time. And rarely did he lose control: it is so easy to make mistakes when you are trying so many things. He made few.' (*Indo-West Indian Cricket*)

Gupte was at his most devastating when New Zealand made their first tour of Pakistan and India in 1955–56. It has to be remembered that New Zealand were possibly the weakest Test nation and could not cope with alien conditions. They lost both series, Gupte at his mesmeric best on easy-paced wickets, capturing 34 wickets for India. Like Ramadhin, he was introduced into the attack at the earliest opportunity, India having no seam bowlers to speak of in those days. Gupte, however, faded from the scene without ever making an impression on the two big powers in Test cricket, England and Australia.

Back to Ramadhin. When the second Test came around English batsmen were in a state of apoplexy. The more Ramadhin was studied the more confusing he became. He went to Lord's confident that England were in the palm of his hand. Once suspicion has taken root in the batsman's mind the bowler is in control. They could not have been more uncertain about Ramadhin if he had been lobbing hand grenades. In 43 overs he took five of England's first innings wickets for 66, striking after Hutton and Washbrook had put on 62 for the first wicket. Both were stumped, Washbrook off the bowling of Ramadhin, Hutton off Valentine, which is a remarkable way for two opening batsmen to get out, especially players of their quality.

A thunderous innings of 168 not out by Walcott was to follow. Goddard declared, setting England 601 to win and Ramadhin and Valentine spun the West Indies to their first-ever Test victory in England. Sonny took 6–86 in 72 overs, 43 of which were maidens. Washbrook dropped anchor for more than an hour at one end against Ramadhin, but despite scoring a century was never quite able to shift the balance of play. Ramadhin eventually bowled him with one that went up the hill. Washbrook utterly misread it.

West Indies won an historic series 3–1, Valentine claiming thirty-three victims and his partner twenty-six. Although England lost the last Test at the Oval by an innings, Hutton carried his bat for 202 in the first innings, defying everything that Ramadhin could muster. It earned him this tribute from Sonny.

'Such a brilliant player. The best I ever bowled to. To score a double century when the ball was turning square was marvellous. Val and me were tops then but we couldn't get him out. I don't think anyone knew my off-break or leg-break. Even Everton Weekes and Clyde Walcott had no idea in the nets. They couldn't pick me out of my hand. They only managed it off the pitch. That's how Hutton started to do it. He played down the wrong line quite a lot but he was so good he survived.'

A year or so later Goddard took his side to Australia for what was expected to be the unofficial championship of the world. There was of course a gross imbalance in their respective firepower. Whereas Australia had Miller and Lindwall in their prime, the West Indies relied heavily on Gerry Gomez and Frank Worrell, both of whom were medium-pacers. Goddard believed Ramadhin and Valentine would be his passport to another record-breaking overseas triumph. He could not have been more wrong, partly because Miller and Hassett declared war on Ramadhin but principally because his big hitters, Walcott and Weekes, were always vulnerable to Miller and Lindwall on the fast Australian wickets.

To begin with Ramadhin's reputation preceded him into the outback and beyond. Who was this Lilliputian with the magical fingers? Even Arthur Mailey, himself an arch-deceiver among googly bowlers, confessed he was unable to work out which way the ball would turn. The Aussies declared that Ramadhin had four different deliveries in his locker: a medium pace off-break which, according to reports, looked for all the world like a leg-break as it left his hand but unaccountably broke back from a foot outside the off-stump; then there was an almost identical delivery which darted back from outside leg-stump; the third was the one Godfrey Evans mentioned which floated higher and hung for a second or two in the air; finally the faster one which ducked in late towards middle and leg. Ramadhin puts it more simply.

'I only had a legger and an off-spinner. Nothing else. I varied the flight and pushed the odd one through a bit quicker. There was no great secret except that I could make every ball look the same. Reporters kept going on about why I had my sleeves buttoned down but there was nothing in that. I think I'm double-jointed but try as I might, my wrist wouldn't turn. It was finger spin with a fast arm action so no one found it easy to pick. I made sure batsmen only had a split second to make up their minds. That's when they make mistakes.'

He was in his element Down Under, although neither he nor Valentine would find the going quite so easy as in England. The Brisbane crowd was instantly on his side during a razor-edge first Test. Ramadhin the batsman playfully took guard a yard outside leg as Lindwall waited to charge in. Forty-six minutes later he was still clowning with 16 runs to his name. But the Ws had failed and West Indies found themselves defending a meagre total of 216. Although he was still only twenty-one, Ramadhin had gained immeasurably in confidence. He taunted Arthur Morris the Australian opening batsman: 'I get you out, Arthur. You not pick the break and you shuffle across the crease.' Later he surprised Hassett and Miller with his gentle 'sledging'. 'I get you, Lindsay. You too short with your reach. And I get you, Keith Miller. You prod forward too far.'

Morris, a belligerent striker of the ball by nature, was sorely perplexed by Ramadhin and forced to curb his natural instincts because he could not detect which way the ball was going to turn. A situation every bowler cherishes. Not only is the batsman guessing what is to come next but the scoreboard has frozen and the pressure to make runs will sooner or later induce a gamble which could prove fatal. Over after over Morris played the ball off the pitch, pinned on to the back foot, jabbing the ball out of his stumps.

At the other end the nimble-footed Hassett tried a different strategy, sallying forth and aiming to play the leg-break through extra-cover. Sadly for him Ramadhin bowled an off-break which nipped through the gap and bowled him.

In the meantime the cat and mouse game between Morris and Ramadhin went on. Here's how the Australian journalist R.S. Whitington described it.

The experienced, thirteen-stone Morris watches the unsophisticated nine-stone Ramadhin like a dog watches a bone. Not once does he make up his mind to make a deliberate stroke but the bowler cannot pierce his vigilant defence. Ramadhin brilliantly fields a scorching drive by the dancing Harvey and raised a roar of applause from a crowd of 21,000 . . . . In his sixth over, Ramadhin, whose control is amazing for a youngster of 21, beats both Morris and Harvey with what were leg-breaks to left-handers. Harvey can make little of either bowler and Morris edges one back just over Ramadhin's head between mid-on and mid-off.

Eventually Morris's patience ran out. He spent nearly two hours accumulating 33 runs before his eagerness not to be dominated by a pocket-sized novice playing only his fifth Test persuaded him to attempt an imprudent half-sweep, half-hook at Valentine. He was caught off a top edge. And so it went: Ramadhin tying them down, Valentine taking the wickets, at least in the first innings. Australians, brought up in the Grimmett/O'Reilly tradition, appreciated the nearest thing they had witnessed to their own two-pronged spin attack. Valentine finished with 5–99, Ramadhin 1–75.

Weekes knuckled down for 70 in the West Indies' second innings but there appeared to be something psychologically wrong with Worrell, who was up against the most persistent and penetrating attack he had ever faced but seemed unable to get his head right. Two years of unbroken cricket without a winter break would not be offered as an excuse today, but in the Australian summer of 1951–52 it was considered an onerous schedule. The upshot was that Australia were set 236 to win. What followed was Ramadhin at his best. R.S. Whitington again:

> . . . the Australian batsmen have little to smile about as they emerge one after another to face the greatest individual bowling performance of the whole series and perhaps the finest individual spin bowling effort seen in Test matches since the days of Bill O'Reilly . . . . Sonny Ramadhin has inherited primarily the Indian outlook on life and Indian charac-teristics. After each day's play most of the West Indies team go back to their hotel for dinner. Sonny is deposited at a Chinese restaurant where he can get his favourite food and, more important still, his rice. More than any other member of the team, he is subject to alternating fits of elation and deep depression.

The Australian media were convinced that if Ramadhin had been removed from the West Indies attack, it would have been taken by the scruff of the neck and collared. In other words, it was because Ramadhin so hypnotized and frustrated the batsmen that Valentine was able to profit. At any rate the Trinidadian oil-field worker with the craving for rice came as close as he could to winning the Test for his country. Under extreme pressure and against players like Morris, Hassett, Harvey, Miller, Hole and Lindwall, Ramadhin returned these figures: 40–9–90–5. He did it on a wicket taking very little turn and clean bowled Harvey, Lindwall and Johnson.

While he wheeled away for most of the innings with Valentine playing second fiddle at the other end, the neurosis in a normally carefree Australian dressing-room was palpable. Top-flight batsmen were arguing among themselves about the best way to combat Ramadhin's bag of tricks – and then changing their minds. Poor Arthur Morris was on the defensive from the word 'Play' because he had given up trying to pick the spin. Harvey, who had neither Morris's defence nor self-discipline, endeavoured to ape the opener's tactics but revised them in the second innings and was still comprehensively outwitted.

Miller, as you might expect, went his own way. He scored 46 in the first innings during which he occasionally took the long handle to Ramadhin and once belted Valentine for 6 over long-on. Miller decided to pursue this course of action further in the second Test at Sydney. It is entirely in keeping with the personality of the larger-than-life all-rounder that he should meet fire with fire. Ramadhin after all was only twenty-two and unaccustomed to the big-match atmosphere. Miller figured there was no way he should be allowed to dominate the way he had at Brisbane and in England a year or so earlier. What's more, the longer he went unpunished the tighter his psychological grip would become. Nobody was sure whether the youngster could withstand an assault or whether he would crack under the strain. Once he cracked there was a very good chance he would stay cracked. That at least was Miller's reasoning. Hassett put his head down and the two of them put on 229, an all-wicket record for Tests between Australia and the West Indies. Miller had the courage of his convictions, driving and cutting both spinners on his way to 129. Australia won by seven wickets, Ramadhin taking 1–196 in the match. He collected five wickets in the fourth Test and pinned batsmen down for lengthy scoreless spells. Overall, though, the series was a major disappointment to the West Indies who wondered whether Ramadhin's reign would evaporate as quickly as it had taken shape. They were reassured in 1954 when he bowled a maiden every three overs and took 23 wickets against England – far more than any bowler on either side.

Observing Ramadhin's progress from a safe distance was Colin

Cowdrey, another prodigy who at the age of twenty-two performed wonders in Australia on Len Hutton's 1954 tour. He was already on the books at Kent while still making the transition from school to Oxford University when Ramadhin first teased England in 1950.

'I remember Cyril Washbrook getting a hundred at Lord's but he had to struggle all the way against Ram and Val. He'd made 110 when Ramadhin bowled a leg-break from the pavilion end. "Washy" was pushing to mid-on but the ball beat the off-stump. I thought: "My God, there's Cyril Washbrook getting it wrong and he's got a century. And to go *up* the hill! Unbelievable." '

By 1957, when John Goddard led the West Indies back to England, Cowdrey was an established member of the England side captained by Peter May. Ramadhin and Valentine, both now twenty-seven years of age, once more seemed to hold the balance of power. If they could burrow into England's minds the way they did in 1950 the West Indies could look forward to more success. It did not work out that way. The Ramadhin problem was settled at Edgbaston in the first Test which proved to be one of the most conclusive of all time.

May was on trial after a drawn series in South Africa:

'We won the first two, drew the third thanks to some ghastly batting by Trevor Bailey, 68 in seven and a half hours, then lost the last two. That wasn't too bad but my batting was. I made one score of 50 in the series and averaged about 13. Although they invited me to lead England in the first Test at Edgbaston there was no promise of any more. I still had a lot to prove against the West Indies.'

He won the toss and chose to bat, resolving to 'have a go' at Ramadhin as soon as he came on. Cowdrey recalls the battle plan.

'We'd heard that Ram didn't bowl so well when you got after him. Keith Miller was the first one to try it in 1952 so we decided the best way to stop him bowling a length was to be bold and take a chance. It wasn't a great success.'

England were shot out for 186 at 3.40 on the first day, Ramadhin claiming 7–49 in 31 overs. He was as enigmatic as ever. There was some damp in the wicket, as the bowler concedes.

'It was a green top and the ball turned. Turned quickly as well. With me being short, my bowling was quite quick and the ball used to skid. There was uncertainty in their eyes. When you see that you capitalize. The batsmen dance to your tune.'

Cowdrey: 'He had a lightning action. Whoosh. Bang! That was his trick. No time to take stock. When he bowled it you wanted to say, "Hold on – can I have that photo taken again please, I wasn't ready!"'

Although I'd been around the Test scene a bit I didn't know where I was against Ramadhin. I never felt so humiliated.'

May: 'Ramadhin was the only bowler I ever faced who gave you no idea which way the ball was going. Like Colin I'd watched him in 1950 when players such as Compton, Washbrook and even Hutton didn't have a clue. He made them look like selling-platers. They'd play one way and the ball would go to the other. Our first innings strategy hadn't worked so we had a rethink. The agreement was to slug it out second time around. We'd play him as an off-spinner and if he bowled the other one and it turned we prayed to God we'd miss it!'

In between, on a wicket playing more and more easily in lovely weather, West Indies went to town. No one enjoyed himself more than Collie Smith, who was to die so tragically in a car accident two years later. There was nothing Trueman, Statham, Laker or Lock could do as he carved himself 161 runs, and Goddard's men were looking down at England from the ramparts of 474 all out. A lead of 288. Typically, Ramadhin had picked up England's first two wickets before the close of play on Saturday. May, coming in at No. 4 after the dismissal of Doug Insole, survived to the rest day but admits that he needed all his mental faculties to avoid despairing at an apparently hopeless state of affairs. The best way, he concluded, was to ignore the truth in the hope that it would go away.

'I told myself not to look at the scoreboard as I went out to bat. I knew we needed 260-odd to avoid an innings defeat but I wasn't anxious to look at the numbers. At that stage it was a question of mind over matter. I remember early in my innings Sonny bowled one on the off-stump. There were a lot of people in the covers but I went through with the shot not knowing whether it was the off-break or not. I middled it and it sailed through extra-cover for 4. I thought: "This isn't too difficult. Perhaps you'd better do it again even though you don't know which way it's going!" My thinking was that a half-volley's a half-volley, so if you're at the pitch of the ball it doesn't matter which way it's spinning. That boundary did me no harm. It was Saturday night and we had the whole of Sunday to think about the situation.'

They could not have imagined the transformation that was now at hand. Cowdrey and May – with maybe a soupçon of generosity from the umpires – pushed the pendulum so far back it very nearly fell off its axle. England did not snatch victory from the proverbial jaws of defeat but they saved a match they seemed guaranteed to lose and in doing so, exorcized the demon in Ramadhin for all time. Cowdrey did it by playing him outside the off-stump with his pads. May relied less on his pads, more on application. The result was a stand of 411 which lasted eight and a quarter hours. It was the biggest of all English test partnerships. Cowdrey contributed 154, May carried his bat for 285. Ramadhin says it was the end of the line.

'They ruined my career. Every time I looked down the wicket at Cowdrey those big pads were coming at me. Wilf Wooller started it that season at Glamorgan and in the county matches after Edgbaston all the players were doing the same. It killed the game. The left leg came right down the wicket and the back leg must have been black and blue from being hit. May was a class batsman but Cowdrey was harder to beat because his bat was so close to his pad. The ball was deceiving them but the wicket got slower. I kept shouting for lbw. Nothing ever happened. One or two would have hit. You couldn't help losing confidence. You go out there to play cricket and all you see is a pad, no bat. It got me down.'

Rohan Kanhai, who deputized behind the stumps for the injured Clyde Walcott, reckoned that at least seven of the one hundred or so lbw appeals were out. There was a similar school of thought among the West Indians in 1950 when Hutton made his double century, as though keeping Ramadhin at bay for so long required divine intervention somewhere along the way. Whereas Cowdrey was learning to fathom Ramadhin during that epic duel, May was no wiser at the end of his innings than he was at the start. Cowdrey first: 'When the radio commentators said Ram's slower ball was the leg-break, word would get back to the bowler via the West Indian dressing-room and Ramadhin would throw in a slower one which was an off-break. Clyde Walcott, who kept wicket in the first innings, used to say he could pick Ramadhin from the boundary. I certainly couldn't. Everton Weekes at slip spread some marvellous humour. When we got it wrong and couldn't conceal our error (which was most of the time) he'd laugh out loud and accuse us of taking the mickey. "I can't believe you really didn't read that," he'd say.

'I promise you it was a nightmare. With his sleeves buttoned to the wrist and his windmill action the ball was on you before you'd seen it leave his hand. After the first few hours I began to pick up something in his action. Gradually from nought out of ten I improved to eight and a half. Almost got to ten except every now and then, just when you thought you had him "sussed", he'd fool you. Ramadhin was an ogre. The rest of the team was out on the balcony when he bowled arguing about who could spot the leg-break from the off-break. Was it the movement of the shoulder which gave it away or was it something else? Fascinating stuff. The crowd was doing the same. Like watching a magician at work. Ram will say he got me out scores of times but he didn't know what was going on in my mind.'

Monday felt like an eternity to May who, remember, was certain to lose the captaincy if his team was humiliated.

'We still had a long way to go without making a mistake. It didn't become any easier because I still couldn't read Ramadhin. We played off the front foot almost exclusively. Even scoring 285 I was still unsure and had to concentrate on every ball. That's what made it so exhausting.'

England could have won the match if they had declared earlier, but the man whose decision it was could barely keep his eyes open. May had to keep checking with the umpires to work out England's lead. He was in no fit state to judge the declaration time.

'I remember Godfrey Evans coming to the wicket on Tuesday morning having been in the pavilion since Saturday afternoon. He said: "Come on skipper, we'll have a few quick runs now!" I said, "It's all right for you to start scampering about – you've been sitting down for three days!" '

May was not the only weary cricketer out there. Ramadhin had bowled a record 98 overs in the second innings. His analysis read 98–35–179–2. Goddard had surely contributed to his demise by over-bowling him. Ram, while refusing to criticize his captain, could hardly turn his arm over by the end of the match. He took only five more wickets in the series, at a cost of 319 runs.

Cowdrey: 'Ram was finished in the next game. Those pitches on which Gilchrist bowled so fast were a graveyard for Ramadhin. Too grassy. You could start to hit through him at Lord's. I got 150 there as well. Those two matches did him.'

He carried on in Australia in 1960 but never had the same success again. Ironically, he made more money playing in the Lancashire leagues where, instead of £15 a Test, it was £1,000 a season. Sonny took 100 wickets most years, had several 10-wicket hauls in an innings and in his last season with Daisy Hill before retiring, he got a hat-trick. All this while running a pub. No wonder he says, 'My legs gave out in the end.'

Trevor Bailey, whose memory is longer than May's, believes Jack Iverson was the only other spin bowler who matched Ramadhin for mystery. The 15-stone Victorian known as 'Australia's Bosanquet' was initially a paceman but developed a unique spinning action which consisted of gripping the ball between his thumb and bent middle finger. Depending on the direction in which his thumb was pointing, Iverson could bowl top-spin, off-spin or leg-spin without any change of action. Alas, his career was a brief one. Having taken 75 wickets for Australia on their New Zealand tour in 1950, and followed it with 6–27 in an innings when England went to Australia the following year, he met his Edgbaston in a state game against New South Wales. Miller and Morris played him into extinction. His 21 Test wickets had cost a mere 15.23 runs each.

That brings us to Bhagwat Chandrasekhar, who deserves a place in the 'Magic Circle' not least because he had the wherewithal to outwit Viv Richards. There is no other bowler in the world who could say that; indeed, of modern spinners possibly he alone ranks alongside Ramadhin as a great deceiver. Chandrasekhar's presence on a cricket field at all was something of a mystery. Why did a man who threw with his left arm bowl with his right? The answer is that Chandra did not have the strength to throw with a right arm withered by polio when he was a child. Bowling he could manage. And how! If Ramadhin was brisk the pencil-slim Indian from Mysore was positively medium-paced. He once bowled a bouncer at Charlie Griffith – and survived to tell the tale. Like Iverson, his stock ball was a googly but batsmen had to watch out for the fizzing top-spinner and the leg-break which turned sufficiently to deceive.

The statistics are impressive: 242 Test wickets at 29.74 and a magnificent contribution to India's first victory in England in 1971 when he took 6–38 to demolish their second innings at the Oval. Such was the confusion he spread that three players, including Ray Illingworth the captain, were caught off full tosses. His match figures at Melbourne seven years later were 12–104 as India recorded their first success in that country too. On top of that, Chandra inspired a series victory over Tony Lewis's touring England team in 1972–73 with a record aggregate of 35 wickets.

It is the effect he had on Viv Richards, however, which most concerns us. Richards admits, 'For a long time I just couldn't deal with Chandra. He flighted the ball so well. He also got turn and bounce. You'd make 30 or 40 runs against him but you could never be sure of getting him under control. Just when you thought you had his measure, he'd produce the ball to trick you. An incredible bowler.'

Most West Indians have trouble with leg-spinners because they like to hit on the up without getting to the pitch of the ball. That's imprudent because the ball is always going to do something. Even

Gary Sobers looked mortal when Bob Barber had a whirl – and Barber was an occasional leg-spinner with Lancashire.

Chandrasekhar put a sign on Richards when the burgeoning West Indian star paid his first visit to India in 1974–75. Clive Lloyd's side collapsed in the first Test at Bangalore after a rain-delayed start on the second day. Eight wickets went for 77, among them Viv Richards mis-hitting to mid-off when Chandra got one to bite sharply. The second innings offered no respite. Again Chandra fooled him, this time having him taken at slip. Four runs in the first innings; three in the second. Richards's emotions were mixed: thoroughly depressed by his failure at the highest level but slightly fearful of the bowler whose spin he could not read and whose flight he could not gauge. Playing forward or back he was at sea – a novel experience for him. Lloyd never had any doubts that he would emerge triumphant: 'Richards was one of the most enthusiastic cricketers I had ever seen and a little impetuous, but he had enormous potential. Even after he failed in the first Test, out both times to Chandrasekhar, we persisted with him because it was obvious he was something special. He rewarded our faith with a magnificent innings at Delhi.'

The West Indies captain played a major part in Richards's instant rehabilitation in the second Test. Having survived a vehement appeal for a catch behind off Chandrasekhar early in the innings, Richards drew more and more confidence from Lloyd's disrespect for the Indian spinners, including Chandra. Using his considerable reach, Lloyd was able to smother the spin of anything full in length. If it dropped short he was murderous. So, in the fullness of time, was Richards. He says, 'It was my first overseas tour for the West Indies and I was naturally nervous. I stood at the other end and watched Lloydie master those guys. It was the most amazing performance I've ever seen.'

Once past his 50, Richards put into practice his firm conviction that slow bowlers should be hammered out of the attack. (Curious in view of his obvious disregard for spinners that he should be one himself.) That Delhi innings eventually closed at 192. It was Richards's first Test century. Once Chandra, Bedi and Prasanna felt the force of his attacking shots they were in full retreat – constrained to change their field placings, obliged to bowl more defensively. In other words the psychological advantage had been grasped by the batsman, for that match at least. Richards never lost his admiration for Chandra.

Ramadhin, Iverson, Qadir, Gupte and Chandrasekhar bamboozled batsmen because they did something different. Jim Laker was the model off-spinner who did not so much bamboozle the Australians as persuade them that he was unplayable. This was a supreme craftsman at work, rather than a sorcerer. Laker could flight his deliveries in and out of nominated holes in the roof of the nets; could hit a florin on the wicket eight times out of ten. The consensus seems to be that the Australians, never happy against off-spin, were out before they were in once the collapse was under way at Old Trafford. The domino effect. That is not to take anything away from Laker who, as well as being a model off-spinner, could extract considerable turn and was a thinking man able to profit from the merest hint of panic in the batting ranks. His captain was Peter May.

'Jim never acknowledged my part in his record. If I hadn't persevered with him he'd never have taken 19 wickets in the match.' An unusual remark but May was only half-joking. 'It was a most extraordinary thing because there were long periods when he didn't bowl at all. I took him off and tried Bailey and Alan Oakman instead. In the meantime Tony Lock was going like a steam train, trying like hell because he didn't like to see Laker get all the wickets. Every time Lock beat the bat he beat everything and everyone else. An inexplicable match. Laker was a very good bowler of course but the Australians seemed haunted. It was all low key. He got a wicket and we said "Well bowled." Nobody hugged him or jumped on him. Jim was phlegmatic. A funny fellow.'

Godfrey Evans has his own view of why Laker set a record which will surely last for ever:

'The Aussies weren't very good at the spinning ball because they'd never had it before. They were jumping about like rabbits, all except for Colin McDonald who played a magnificent innings of 80-odd. They could hear the ball buzzing in the air when Jim released it. That was enough to terrify anyone. With his action of tossing the ball high into the air he fooled them into coming forward to play only to find it wasn't there. So they'd take half a step further and still the ball wasn't where they thought. He had this big forefinger which he'd wrap around the ball and make it turn sometimes six inches. The next one was delivered with the same action but didn't spin anything like as much. Jim would never tell us how he did it. Very secretive. I suppose that was part of his magic. The Aussies just didn't know what to make of him. Our batsmen might have handled him better, but don't forget Jim took 8–2 in a Test trial at Bradford back in 1950. It wasn't just the spin which did the Aussies at Old Trafford. It was the aura of the man. He was the only person who looked like getting wickets. I remember Tony Lock catching one at short leg and cursing under his breath:

"Well bowled, you bastard!" He was so angry he bowled faster and faster and that meant he was inclined to pull it down a bit so they were getting shorter and shorter. Whistling past McDonald's nose! Tony lost his temper. You mustn't do that at cricket.'

On the distinguished list of bowlers who had taken most wickets in a Test match, a surprising name inserted itself just below Laker and Sydney Barnes, surprising because hardly anyone except the members of Northamptonshire 2nd XI had heard of him: Robert Arnold Lockyer Massie. I do him a disservice. Kilmarnock Cricket Club in Scotland had engaged him for three years before Colin Milburn noticed him bowling in his native Western Australia and recommended the medium-pacer to Northants. 'It was a wet summer and the ball was always wet in your hands,' says Massie, who did not enjoy his trial period with the second team. 'I took 3–166 in two matches so they said, "Don't ring us, we'll ring you." Can't blame 'em, really.'

In the summer of 1972, Ray Illingworth's befuddled England team came reeling back to the Lord's pavilion like a succession of drunks wondering, 'Who is this guy?' Massie was making his Test debut for Ian Chappell's Australians who were already one down in the series. On the face of it, a fairly innocuous opening bowler. If there was to be any menace it was more likely to come from the other end where the twenty-two-year-old Dennis Lillee was raw and hungry. England were nonplussed when Massie went around the wicket to John Edrich and decided to stay there. He startled them with a display of swing bowling not witnessed before or since. The ball boomeranged both ways, and none of the England players could read him. With a wrist spinner that is not uncommon, but it is virtually unheard of for a medium-pacer to disguise his inswinger and outswinger with such subtlety that no one can tell them apart. In excellent conditions for swing bowling, Massie took 8–84 followed by 8–53. Not surprisingly Australia squared the series at one each, and with match figures of 16–137 the former bank teller from Perth went third behind Laker and Barnes in the world records.

John Edrich prides himself on being clean bowled so few times. Massie found a way through. 'He was letting it go as the away swinger but it came back at me, took the inside edge and knocked back the middle stump. I remember thinking, "Where the hell did that come from?" I'd never seen anyone swing the ball as much as that. Incredible because it moved so late. The funny thing is that I fancied my chances against him like mad. If he'd been a bit quicker he wouldn't have been so effective because you'd have been less inclined to go after him.'

Even the multi-experienced Edrich did not learn his lesson. He gave Massie the charge in the second innings and was stumped.

Inquests and running analyses occupied television commentators and players alike as Massie's fleeting moment on the world stage unfolded before their disbelieving eyes. One of the most troubled spectators was Illingworth, the England captain.

'It was the greenest wicket I'd ever seen. There were green skid marks about two feet long all over it. Snowy or Geoff Arnold would have got 5–20 each on that. Massie bowled two different inswingers, which was the main problem. Most of us could tell the big in-ducker but the one which only came in six inches must have been delivered with a turn of the wrist. People said you shouldn't get out to someone bowling round the wicket, but an inswinger from round was a straight ball by the time it reached you; you had to play it. He also bowled a very good outswinger which started outside leg-stump and kept going. Catches to the slips were carrying chest high because there was so much juice in the wicket.'

Massie: 'I didn't go out there expecting to get sixteen wickets. Like a footballer scoring a hat-trick you can't pre-plan. It either happens or it doesn't. I went round the wicket to bowl at Edrich and stayed there because it worked. The conditions certainly helped but they kept playing balls they shouldn't have. They played pretty badly. I've bowled as well as that and got nothing. It was the angle that beat them. Sure I tried to camouflage what I was doing but there's only so much you can do. I could bowl an inswinger side-on but never managed to bowl a proper outswinger open-chested. That would've been quite something! With a swing bowler it's the follow-through that really gives it away but it's too late by then. The mental process can't cope with that.'

England were in such disarray that Illingworth, reading allegations by Ted Dexter in the *Sunday Mirror* that Massie had been using lip-salve to polish one side of the ball in the Lord's and Trent Bridge Tests, performed a little experiment at Headingley. He took Basil D'Oliveira, Tony Greig and Chris Old to the nets, gave them each three balls shined with lip-salve (lip-ice as he calls it) and three ordinary balls and instructed them to bowl. His conclusion?

'The difference was remarkable. The polished ball swung twice as much. I'm sure some of that must have been going on.'

Edrich was not party to the experiments but refused to believe that anyone – least of all an unheard-of bowler who disappeared as fast as he came – could swing the ball so far, unaided. 'Nothing much happened before tea then Massie came on after the interval and it went like a boomerang again. It was never proved but one side of that ball was like glass. That's how he did it.'

Massie laughs off the suggestion to this day. 'Lip-salve? Never heard of it. I guess those Poms would have to find some excuse!'

'The amazing thing,' says Illingworth, 'is that Dennis Lillee was at the other end. He got the first two wickets in each innings and that was all. He was pitching off-and-middle and missing everything going up the hill so you can imagine how much he was doing. At his pace none of us could lay a bat on him.'

Whatever the truth of the matter, Lord's 1972 was the scene of one of the biggest enigmas in Test history. Massie's Test career was equally puzzling. It spanned 191 days and six Tests. In the remaining five his aggregate was only fifteen wickets. At the time of writing he is a cricket commentator with the Australian Broadcasting Commission:

'I lost it in the West Indies. Had to change my style and try to bang the ball in. It didn't work. I was dropped after two more Tests against Pakistan. Then Western Australia dropped me too. Gradually I realized there was more to life than cricket and packed it in.'

THREE

The Fury

'Meet it and you do not see its face.
Follow it and you do not see its back.'
LAO TZU

Ken Barrington was doing his best to enjoy the swordfish steak as we relaxed in downtown Port of Spain. Relaxed, did I say? Kenny rarely switched off to that extent. Had he been able to anticipate a fraction of what lay ahead of us on that tour he would have been on the plane home before the dessert trolley reached us. Sadly, he never did come home. Kenny knew Caribbean cricket well. It was grim in his day when Charlie Griffith was uprooting batsmen with kink-armed yorkers and Wes Hall was trying to break the sound barrier. Now it was a good deal more unwholesome. (A bit like the swordfish steak.) Clive Lloyd wanted a West Indies victory more fervently than any previous Caribbean captain. If a few heads and hearts were broken along the way, well so be it. He had four furious fast men to unleash and rotate. It would be a miracle if England were not humiliated.

The mental wearing-down process was all too familiar to Kenny. 'Every part of their game is negative. They would rather ping it around your ears than bowl it at your stumps. You get so few overs in a day and so few balls an over to score off that the chances of making 250 are tiny. And if you don't make at least 250 in reasonable time how can you ever win a match?'

Only by giving them the same treatment. But where did England have the bowlers to compare with Roberts, Holding, Croft and Garner?

The agonies of that 1981 tour would exact the maximum toll on England's assistant manager. They also brought to a premature end Botham's stewardship of the team. Ill-conceived as it possibly was to nominate him, the selectors had few alternatives after Mike Brearley called it a day. Brearley realized after a 3–0 defeat in post-Packer Australia that it was a good time to go. Little did he know he would be back.

International cricket had gone full circle since 1932–33. Douglas Jardine's men bowled what was euphemistically termed 'leg theory'. Lloyd's warriors were bowling 'throat theory'. Clive would not put it this way but the aim was identical – to intimidate, restrict opportunities to score and make batting a downright unpleasant business. The difference is that Jardine had something approaching a pretext. Don Bradman was a pain in the rump. As expected he took English bowling apart on the 1930 tour, beginning with a double century in the opening fixture at Worcester and continuing with a masterful 254 in the Lord's Test. He averaged 139 in the series. You did not have to be a clairvoyant to see that this sphinx-like man with no apparent flaw in his technique would make bowling a depressing prospect for many years. That is, unless something dramatic was dreamed up to stop him. Necessity being the mother of invention, Jardine came up with Bodyline (a name coined by the opposition) which achieved everything it set out to do.

Lloyd had no such problems. Most of the world's devastating batsmen were in his own team. The only Bradmanesque figure was India's Sunil Gavaskar who, paradoxically, handled the four-pronged pace battery as well as anyone.

Interestingly, the players returning from the Bodyline tour had a team meeting at which it was agreed leg theory was unplayable. If three chaps were bowling Bodyline what was the point of playing cricket? The game would suffer a huge tilt of balance. Furthermore spectators would be alienated if not enraged (they already had been) and physical harm could follow. They determined to put Jardine's scheme back in its coffin. Cricket's administrators inserted the Intimidation Clause to the law governing Fair and Unfair Play and that seemed to be the end of the matter. From time to time wild young things would try to revive the principle if not the name, but most captains nipped it in the bud. Then came Lloyd's West Indies. Gradually at first with Boyce, Holder and Julien, then stepping up the tempo with Daniel and Roberts, Holding, Garner and Croft, Marshall, Patterson, Walsh, Bishop and Ambrose. Not that life had been much calmer when Sobers came on as first change after Hall and Griffith. Colin Cowdrey doubts whether anyone nowadays bowls any faster than Wes but has noticed a distinct shortage of brotherly love through the 1970s and 1980s.

'You expect short balls, especially in the Caribbean. Now they're trying to improve their line of shortness. It's calculated aggression. You don't get just the occasional one which might break your arm.

There are several balls an hour like that. Cricket is all the poorer for it. What people seem to have forgotten is that when we were shaving in the morning or having breakfast, we used to get as uptight about facing Ramadhin and Valentine or Benaud and Tayfield as they do about pacemen today. The science has gone. Throat bowling's not a science. When Gary Sobers turned to spin and he and Lance Gibbs bowled twenty-two overs an hour at you in terrible heat, that was good tactics. They kept you playing and playing and playing. You wanted to plead for time to think about what you were doing. There was no chance. You'd get a ball on a perfect length here, another one there, then they'd turn you around quickly for the next over. It was breathless cricket. That's what I call clever psychology. These days you only get a dozen overs an hour. Time to read a book in between!'

A batsman with too much time on his hands, however, can be under as much pressure. Edrich, bat on hip, patience stretched like piano wire, would wait for what seemed like an age for Lillee or Thomson or Hall or Griffith to get back to their marks. In 1976 at Trent Bridge, it was Holding and Roberts bearing down upon England. David Steele and Edrich had a mid-wicket conversation as Steele came in to bat.

'How are you getting on?' asked Steele.

'I've never been so bored in all my life,' Edrich replied. 'Five balls out of six are too wide to hit. Can't see the point in this!'

Therein, a grave danger. Boredom has a knack of inviting lapses in concentration. Against the world's fastest bowlers you cannot afford too many of those.

Clive Lloyd is, on the face of it, a gentle giant. Quietly spoken, mild mannered and, like most West Indians, good to his mother. But not far beneath that soft exterior is a tough shell. Not far behind that bashful smile is a grim determination to succeed more associated with the Australians. Lloyd was disgusted at the lukewarm reaction from the West Indies Cricket Board when he captained them to World Cup triumph in 1975.

'The team members never received any recognition from the Board, apart from the £350 fee which had been agreed. We were left feeling bitter. There was no ceremony, nothing until the Guyanese government flew me home with the Cup. We had a procession through the streets of Georgetown and all the players were presented with gold chains. I can just imagine what they'd have done in India, Pakistan or Australia if *they'd* won.'

The Board was more interested in filling the coffers, and agreed to bring forward the West Indies tour of Australia which would now begin later the same year. Naturally the prospect of the world champions confronting Ian Chappell's beaten finalists on Aussie soil aroused enormous passion. It also proved to be a watershed in modern cricket, the tour which planted in Lloyd's mind the thought that an artillery of spiteful pace bowlers was the passport to world domination. Unfortunately for the rest of the world, there was no cricketing nation better equipped to provide them and go on providing them.

Contrary to expectations, West Indies were humiliated 5–1 in a money-spinning six-Test series hurriedly arranged to replace the cancelled South African tour. Australia won the first Test by eight wickets at Brisbane after Lloyd's team lost six for 99 before lunch. One of them was Viv Richards, caught at slip off Lillee for a duck. It was a preview of what was to come as Lillee and Thomson (after a slow start) blitzed the world champions. Says Richards:

'I'd never seen a wicket play that quickly in my life . . . . It was an unbelievable scene. I was totally overcome by the whole occasion.'

Richards went back to the drawing board. This was the toughest cricket he had ever seen, entirely foreign to the West Indian nature although it would play a large part in shaping his approach to cricket. 'If you were confident, you'd survive; if not, Lillee and Thomson would terrify you out of the game. They were the toughest competitors of the lot. The first time we played against them we tried to take the attack to them. They ran all over us. It's the Australian way of playing cricket. Perhaps they've never forgotten the battles against England in the old Bodyline days and decided never to be subjected to that kind of thing again.'

Thanks to a sensational innings of 169 by Roy Fredericks, to 149 by Lloyd who stood back to cut and pull the pacemen to their consternation, and to some searing pace from Holding and Roberts who took seven second-innings wickets, West Indies suggested temporarily at Perth that they might make a series of it. But it was not to be. Lillee and Thomson, backed up by Walker and Gilmour, blew them away. Lloyd scored another century at Melbourne and found a way of counteracting the Australian bombardment, but he was unable to raise the spirits of a demoralized outfit. The series was settled by an explosive burst from Thomson in the fourth Test at Sydney. He collected six wickets in a spell which broke West Indian resistance once and for all. They had no stomach for the remaining two Tests and could not wait to get home. In the light of what we have seen since, it is hard to imagine West Indian cricketers so comprehensively outgunned. It hurt Lloyd deeply.

'Thomson and Lillee were the best combination of fast bowlers any captain could hope to have. None of our batsmen had come across bowling of such speed before and they were always under pressure in the first innings. Middle-order batsmen had to face Thomson and Lillee in their opening spells with the ball still new. Several of them got hit. I was hit on the jaw by Lillee in Perth and by Thomson in Sydney. Bernard Julien had his thumb and Kallicharran had his nose broken. All of us felt the pain of a cricket ball thudding into our bodies at 90 m.p.h. It takes a lot of courage to stand up to the threat of physical danger.'

Gnawing at the West Indies captain was the way his team had disintegrated to such an extent that it was impossible to motivate them for the second half of the tour. This went against everything he had tried so hard to eliminate from the West Indian psyche.

'I was tired of hearing that we were a bunch of Calypso cricketers who couldn't put it together, nice guys who caved in when the going got tough. I wanted the world to know we weren't pushovers but a highly professional outfit. That tour of Australia set us back a long way. It set me thinking all over again.'

Despite everything, Lloyd, Fredericks, Richards and Kallicharran had demonstrated magnificent courage and technique against the dreaded Lillee and Thomson who had aleady created such havoc against England. For now, Lloyd's burgeoning belief in an all-pace attack was fertilized when Bishen Bedi took the Indians to the Caribbean early in 1976. Curiously the West Indian spinners, Jumadeen and Holford, were largely responsible for winning the first Test of a series which would herald their demise. And in Barbados of all places. By the second Test in Trinidad, India were sounding a warning. Gavaskar and Patel each scored centuries and West Indies narrowly saved the match.

So we come to the match which changed the face of Test cricket for the next fifteen years at least. By chance it too was played at Port of Spain because Georgetown, Guyana was under flood. Lloyd was dismayed at having to play in Trinidad again. He thought it was the only place India stood a chance of winning. They did, Lloyd setting them 406 to win with one day and a session left. He had miscalculated. 'Michael Holding bowled really fast in the first innings and India struggled to 228, so I didn't think they had a chance of getting more than 400 to win.'

The only team to achieve that distinction had been Bradman's Australians in 1948. The wicket was lifeless. Holding could get nothing out of it, so Lloyd, for the first and last time in his career, placed his reliance on spin to undo the opposition. Partly because he handles it so well as a batsman and partly because no spinner of world-beating stature had emerged since the retirement of his cousin Lance Gibbs the previous year, Lloyd seldom saw spin as a potent attacking weapon.

'We had to rely on three spinners to give us victory and it never crossed my mind we wouldn't make it. I was furious when I saw they weren't up to it. There's no way India should have won from that position.'

It had been an experimental attack, both Padmore and Imtiaz Ali playing their first Tests. Their figures had Lloyd tearing out his hair: Padmore 47–10–98–0; Jumadeen 41–13–70–2 and Ali 17–3–52–0.

'We decided to bring in an extra paceman for the last Test in Jamaica. Out went Ali and Padmore and in came Wayne Daniel to join Holding, Julien and Holder. Some people said Frank Worrell might have played four pacemen at some time, I'm not sure. I don't see anything wrong with it. In the same period Australia had Lillee, Thomson, Walker and Gilmore with Ashley Mallett as the one spinner. That was quite successful and England have copied it ever since.'

The final Test was as farcical as it was unsavoury, with the four fast men in lethal form on a distinctly unpleasant wicket. Bedi declared the Indian first innings closed at 306–6 in order to protect his lower-order batsmen. They had been 136 without loss when Lloyd resorted to intimidatory methods. Viswanath was caught off a ball from Holding which broke his hand and Gaekwad, who stood up to the battering for a day, was finally put in hospital by the same bowler. The ball struck him over the ear after he had made an extremely brave 81 and he was detained in Kingston hospital for several days. Patel was hit in the mouth by a ball from Holder as the catalogue of injuries became more and more severe.

On the rest day the Indian manager, Polly Umrigar, called the match a 'war' and accused Holding of intimidatory bowling. Lloyd, while confessing he felt a certain sympathy with the tourists, was and is unrepentant.

'Cricket's not an easy game, and why should it be? I wear glasses so I'm more vulnerable than most. I've gone through the mill with them all. The Indians only had themselves to blame for backing away and taking their eyes off the ball. You've got to be tough if you want to get through this world no matter what you do. The Indians blamed us for their own deficiencies. If I'd been that afraid, I wouldn't have been playing cricket for a living.'

Defiant stuff from a defiant character who thought West Indies cricket had been sloppily led too often in the past by Sobers. Lloyd provoked dark mutterings about Bodyline when he encouraged Holding to bowl around the wicket, changing direction against batsmen who were failing to get in line.

The upshot was that India batted five men short in their second innings. This was the miserable scorecard which enabled West Indies to win by ten wickets and capture the series:

Gavaskar c Julien b Holding	2
Vengsarkar lbw b Jumadeen	21
Amarnath st Murray b Jumadeen	60
Madan Lal b Holding	8
Venkataraghavan b Holding	0
Kirmani not out	0
Gaekwad absent hurt	
Viswanath absent hurt	
Bedi absent hurt	
Chandrasekhar absent hurt	
Patel absent hurt	
Extras (nb 6)	6
Total	97

The last word belonged to Gavaskar, but the last act in a particularly nasty and dangerous period of Test cricket has still to be played: 'Short-pitched bowling at that speed is barbaric.'

And referring to the Jamaican crowd who, he claimed, had chorused, 'Kill him, maan!' at every delivery, Gavaskar added, 'Those people belong to the jungles and the forest instead of a civilized country.'

While I do not propose that Lloyd derived any pleasure from the Indian casualty list, there is no doubt that he was now as certain as Jardine had been forty-four years earlier that pace would break down the strongest barrier. The West Indians themselves had flinched and succumbed to Lillee and Thomson, Bradman was shaken by Larwood, so to hell with diplomacy, let's put West Indian cricket where it belongs. What he had seen the Indians doing, backing away to leg, was exactly what Bob Wyatt, the England captain, had noticed during the Oval Test in 1930. Rain had given the wicket extra zip which was exploited by Maurice Tate and Larwood for two hours the next morning. Archie Jackson dealt with it a good deal more comfortably than Bradman. Wyatt said this: 'We discussed on the voyage how we would get Bradman out. That's when fast-leg theory was first mentioned. It was quite obvious that Bradman didn't like it. He drew away, didn't cope with it very well at all.'

The Don made 232 at the Oval before he was controversially caught behind off Larwood. It was the first time in eight Test matches that the England demon had captured his wicket. Be that as it may, Larwood had been quick to spot the disturbance in Bradman's equanimity. 'He murdered us in that series but I saw him definitely flinching at the Oval. The other lad, Archie Jackson, never flinched once. Bradman showed distrust of the short ball.'

The tilt in equilibrium was about to take place, as it has many times down the years whenever the bat has dominated the ball for too long. Although spin bowlers have had an impact, it has almost always been speed which has broken the stranglehold. Not reckless speed – Larwood had to be at his most accurate to bowl to a field of five men clustered in the short-leg area – but speed with a constant hint of menace which has the batsman preoccupied with three thoughts: how to defend his wicket, how to score, and how to avoid injury. Even Bradman was unnerved by that although to be fair he did average 56.57 in the Bodyline series, topping the Australian averages. He told me:

'To participate in Test cricket obviously places a strain on an individual and it always demanded a calm approach, which I believe I had. Bodyline was disturbing. It created a new dimension in that physical protection of one's person became a prime necessity as distinct from the normal process of defending one's wicket and scoring runs. It generated ill feeling between teams quite out of character with normal cricket.'

Bradman developed the counteraction he had flirted with at the Oval – moving outside the leg stump to hit the ball through the comparatively vacant off-side. 'When you have seven men on the leg side, plus the bowler and the wicket-keeper, there is no future in hitting the ball there. It was technically wrong to move outside the leg stump as well as being difficult and dangerous. Contrary to what some people were saying, it exposed me to greater danger because instead of moving inside the line of the ball, I was moving into it. I didn't make a great success of it. It was a pretty impossible task.'

Wisden described the third Test in Adelaide as 'probably the most unpleasant ever played' although it may have been eclipsed by Jamaica 1976. There cannot however have been many more blatant acts of intimidation than Jardine's tactics after Billy Woodfull was hit over the heart by a short one from Larwood. No sooner had the batsman recovered from a sickening blow which enraged the crowd than the England captain moved all his orthodox off-side fielders to leg. It seems on the face of it an astonishingly tactless and insensitive thing to do but then Jardine was determined to win the series at any price. Little wonder the authorities marshalled a large detachment of mounted police behind the Adelaide pavilion in case Bradman was hit and all hell let loose.

Most of the MCC players incidentally agreed that Woodfull had been the architect of his own misfortune, ducking into a reasonably good length ball. Larwood appealed for lbw and insists to this day that the ball would have knocked out middle stump. Bert Sutcliffe took a similar view and believed the Australians made altogether too much of a song and dance about Jardine's methods. 'Their tactics were completely wrong, especially Woodfull's. Whenever anything was pitched short he went down on his hands and knees hoping it would bounce over the stumps. He was hit on the backside several times. Jardine got a raw deal, so did Larwood.'

Jardine clearly regretted nothing, believed he had achieved what he set out to do and defended the use of hostile measures in what, to him, was a form of warfare. Cricket, he said, was a 'peculiarly English heritage' whose only worthy definition was the following (first coined by a New Zealander): 'That beautiful, beautiful game which is battle and service and sport and art.'

To his credit, the fearsomely maligned Jardine scored a century when the West Indies bowlers Martindale and Constantine were instructed to give him a dose of his own medicine at Old Trafford the following summer. Hammond had his chin cut open in the same game. That match effectively marked the end of Bodyline.

The next fast bowling wave brought us Ray Lindwall and Keith Miller who teamed up after the Second World War. Lindwall, like Larwood under six feet tall, had tried to model himself on the England bowler who made such an impression on the young boy with his 33 wickets on that controversial tour. It was not long before Lindwall had top-flight batsmen hopping about in the crease as he cut a swathe through England on Bradman's last tour of 1948. Denis Compton suffered a cut above his eye mis-hooking and Jack Robertson was hospitalized with a damaged jaw. There was of course much more to Lindwall than naked hostility. In 1953 he delivered a memorable over to one of England's finest post-war batsmen, Peter May, who was on the verge of a permanent England place when Surrey played the visiting Australians.

'He was moving it away late both ways and beat me completely with at least four balls. Ray was the best bowler I faced by a mile. It was always a struggle and probably because of that over I only played in the first and last Tests of the series.'

Miller was the *real* demon. Unpredictable; frequently more concerned with the three o'clock winner at Thirsk than the state of the game and at his most threatening after a skinful the night before. Compton did not scare easily but confesses he was a regular visitor to the men's room before going out to face his old adversary. They met when Miller, stationed with the Royal Australian Air Force in England, was playing a charity match at Lord's:

'I was getting among the runs when the ball was thrown as a last resort to a tall chap with brushed-back hair who had been racing round the boundary like a young gazelle, drawing roars of applause for his fielding. I was told he wasn't really a bowler but wanted a bit of exercise. When he let the ball go he was so quick my hair stood on end.'

Miller was not always highly motivated. As good as he was, he did not like bowling as much as batting. Bradman once asked him to bowl on the 1948 tour and had the ball tossed back at him by Miller who shouted, 'No thanks. Find someone else!' Their relationship was strained. When he did bowl he was as fearsome as Lindwall. When England squared the 1954–55 series 1–1, Hutton tried his utmost to miss the third Test. Godfrey Evans could not believe it.

'He was a great captain, but he was scared. Nerves had got to him. Bill Edrich broke the news. He said, "Have you heard about Len? He doesn't want to play. Says he's got the flu. Come on, Godders, get the bugger out of bed!" We decided it didn't matter whether he had the flu or not, he *had* to captain the team. It was a psychological thing. Having just won the Sydney Test we couldn't go to Melbourne without our captain and best player. We talked him out of it, got him dressed and carted him down. He was more worried about Miller than the flu.'

The big Victorian was all in favour of bouncing batsmen, so keen was he to discourage the return of the heavy scorers typified by Bradman, Ponsford, Hammond and Hutton. Ponsford in particular made cricket look hopelessly one-sided. Between 1922 (when he scored 429 for Victoria against Tasmania) and his retirement in 1934, he had thirteen scores over 200 including two over 300 and a second 400. Says Miller:

'For almost twenty years the giants waged a private run-scoring war, victories being registered as cold figures beside their names on the cricket scorebook. Later those figures were to prove a barrier to friendship . . . . The century, once the hallmark of the master batsmen, lost its worth. As Ponsford, Bradman and Hammond reached the century, they merely acknowledged the crowd's applause, touched the peak of their cap and settled down for a second hundred.'

As aggressive as he was, Miller was the first to buy his opponent a pint after the game and deplored the animosity created by Jardine's and Lloyd's regimes. 'Do we want another Bradman era? Certainly cricket produced record gates and dazzling batting from one or two individuals but it almost brought about the cessation of Anglo-Australian tests when Bodyline was introduced to combat one man's undoubted genius. Then cricket lost its real value as a sport. It became a war.'

Hutton longed for the time when England would have a genuine 'quick' with whom to answer the bombardment of Lindwall and Miller. In 1952 the irrepressible Fred Trueman came bursting out of the Pennines, all brimstone, flapping shirtsleeves and bandy legs. His later opening partnership with the rubber-jointed Brian Statham owed nothing to Bodyline. It was a different philosophy. Statham would argue that there was no point wasting energy on deliveries which climbed chest high when he would much sooner hit the stumps. For one glorious year during the Statham/Trueman era Frank Tyson shocked Australia into submission on Hutton's tour of 1954–55. Tyson was not able to make more than a brief impression on the world scene because his limbs let him down. It was however a lasting impression of a big man with a raking stride who probably bowled as fast as anyone before or since. Hutton was tired of being on the receiving end and decided to fight fire with fire. Leaving Trueman at home, probably for diplomatic reasons, he set sail with the four-pronged pace battery of Statham, Tyson, Loader and Bailey. The result was that Hutton became the first captain in thirty years to retain the Ashes after winning them in England. Also on that tour – his first at the tender age of twenty – was Colin Cowdrey.

'The amazing thing was that two of the world's finest fast bowlers never enjoyed bowling bouncers. Statham dropped the odd one short of a length to keep the batsman alert, but no more. Tyson just occasionally let a bouncer go but somehow it was irrelevant. What he was really after was the yorker. The whole *raison d'être* of bowling was different. It was as though Concorde hadn't been thought of, only

VC10s. Brian and Frank went to bed at night dreaming of pitching middle and leg, making it straighten, holding the seam up. Hitting the stumps or getting a nick to the keeper was the real joy.'

This is how Tyson, a graduate from Durham University who recited Wordsworth to himself while walking back to his bowling mark, described the business of fast bowling in his autobiography *A Typhoon called Tyson*:

> To bowl quick is to revel in the glad arrival action; to thrill in physical prowess and to enjoy a certain sneaking feeling of superiority over the other mortals who play the game. No batsman likes quick bowling and this knowledge gives one a sense of omnipotence.

He was left without any senses at all in the second Test at Sydney when a bouncer from Lindwall, who was retaliating to one he had earlier received from the Englishman, hit Tyson on the back of the head. It took a long time to get him back on his feet and back to the dressing-room. This is how Hutton recalled the aftermath in his book *Fifty Years of Cricket*:

> When he came out of his concussed state I swear there was a new light in his eye ... I'm not given to fanciful imagination, and the fact is that when he bowled the next day he was a yard, maybe a yard and a half faster than before ... When Lindwall came in to bat Tyson was bowling. A flashpoint situation. Everyone on the ground, probably including Lindwall, expected Tyson to finger the bump on his head and let fly a retaliatory bumper. Instead, Frank slipped in the perfect, spot-on yorker which utterly deceived and bowled Lindwall.

The England captain takes the credit for persuading Tyson to reduce his run-up after an innocuous performance (29–1–160–1) in the steamy heat of Brisbane where the first Test was played. Tyson was wilting after four overs and Hutton figured his main warhead would be washed up before the series got going: hence the shorter run. 'The results exceeded our expectations. After he was streamlined he lost none of his pace and gained in accuracy.'

The two men, northerners both, developed the sort of friendship and understanding that Hutton and Trueman were unable to achieve in the early days. Fred never really forgave his Yorkshire county colleague for leaving him out of the tour party and the relationship took a long time to recover.

The Australians had the Melbourne wicket watered during the third Test but the plot backfired hopelessly. An inexperienced groundsman put the sprinklers on the arid Melbourne wicket and discovered to his horror that it was still wet the next morning after the rest day. Because the authorities stayed silent, false rumours about a conspiracy began to emerge.

It was all a ghastly mistake. Tyson produced his most furious spell of the series, taking 7–27 in the second innings as England won by 128 runs. The turning point was Godfrey Evans's catch to dismiss Neil Harvey when the great Australian left-hander had made 11. Godfrey spent the entire series taking the ball airborne or diving sideways:

'He wasn't a great bowler but he was the fastest thing we'd seen. I was twenty yards back and still jumping high. They'd almost have gone for six byes if I hadn't reached them. It was a pleasure to stand there when Keith Miller came in to bat. The conversation went like this:

' "Morning Godfrey."

' "Morning Keith.'

' "I hope that bastard comes off soon!"

'We hadn't been able to frighten Keith before.

'Neil Harvey was batting on the last morning and they wanted 100-odd to win with eight wickets left. Frank's second ball was quick down the leg side and I saw Neil move to guide it down. It went a bit uppishly and I thought, "Bloody hell, Godders, why didn't you have a go for it?" As luck would have it, Frank did exactly the same thing off the fourth ball and Neil played exactly the same shot. Of course I was ready for it. I dived full length and got my hand to it. Colin Cowdrey was fielding at short-leg and I nearly landed on his toes.'

Australia, beaten 3–1 at home, were demoralized just as the West Indies would be when they walked into the Lillee/Thomson whirlwind and just as successive England teams would be when confronted by Holding, Roberts, Marshall and company. There is no doubt some truth in this post mortem by Ian Johnson, the Australian captain in 1954–55, but the dividing line between irresistible bowling and abject batting is a very fine one. The anatomy of any batting collapse must necessarily involve a lemming factor. The sight of colleagues following each other back to the pavilion with monotonous regularity is more than likely to induce a feeling of helplessness – a feeling that no matter what you do you cannot reverse the trend. At any rate, Johnson was in no doubt that his men were conquered as much by psychology as anything else.

'We failed because our batsmen gave one of the most gutless exhibitions seen in a Test series . . . I refuse to believe occasions did not arise when the batsmen went down without showing their customary and expected fight. Their morale was low because they forgot the

ENGLAND v AUSTRALIA
Melbourne 1955

AUSTRALIA SECOND INNINGS

Favell	b Appleyard	30
Morris	c Cowdrey b Tyson	4
Benaud	b Tyson	22
Harvey	c Evans b Tyson	11
Miller	c Edrich b Tyson	6
Hole	c Evans b Statham	5
Archer	b Statham	15
Maddocks	b Tyson	0
Lindwall	lbw b Tyson	0
Johnson	not out	4
Johnston	c Evans b Tyson	0
	Extras	14
	Total	111

Bowling: Tyson 12.3–1–27–7
  Statham 11–1–38–2

meaning of courage or, if they did not forget the meaning of it, they forgot how to apply it.'

The Typhoon eventually broke a bone in his left foot, exactly as Larwood had done. Because his foot splayed out in the delivery stride, the accident was not unexpected. Curiously, like Larwood he also settled in Australia, both of them welcomed into the bosom of a nation they had each terrorized in their different ways.

The fear factor in cricket has developed in a haphazard fashion. Fred Spofforth, the Dennis Lillee look-alike, and Charles Kortright both bowled like greased lightning in the nineteenth century but seemed more intent on hitting the stumps than putting the fear of God into their opponents. Gilbert Jessop, better known for taking a bludgeon to bowlers who tried to pin *him* down, was also an opening bowler for England at the turn of the century and revelled in hostility. So much so that the word 'helmet' first appeared in a limerick devoted to his bloodthirsty antics in the Varsity match of 1896. Jessop attacked the Oxford batsmen with a constant fusillade of bouncers delivered from around the wicket. Several players were injured and his own wicket-keeper was knocked out:

'There was a young fresher called Jessop
Who was pitching 'em less up and less up,
'Till one of the pros
Got a blow on the nose
And said: "In a helmet I'll dress up!" '

A couple of years before the Bodyline tour, Learie Constantine was the forerunner of the modern West Indian paceman, blinding pace combined with aggression. Too much for England. In Guyana in 1930 he took nine wickets in the match when West Indies won a Test for the first time. In his book *The Fast Men* David Frith describes the way Constantine jolted England out of their cosy complacency:

> . . . he presented a fearful sight to an England XI many of whom were beyond the first flush of youth. Teeth flashing, he bounded in and bowled bouncer after bouncer, with only two men on the off side . . . George Gunn, then having turned fifty, made 35 as opener adopting tactics all his own: to Constantine he advanced down the pitch before the ball was bowled and played short deliveries with a dead-bat shoulder high . . . The situation exploded eventually when the batsman was hit painfully under the armpit.

Constantine was ahead of his time. Short-pitched stuff, close fielders in an arc on the leg-side. Bodyline before the name was thought of. Bob Wyatt, who was soon to notice Bradman's evident dislike for the short-pitched ball, underwent a fearsome initiation ceremony himself when Constantine played against his county, Warwickshire in 1928. Not only did Wyatt have to stomach the grisly sight of his colleague Len Bates carried unconscious from the field after being poleaxed by a bouncer, but he stood helpless as the first two balls he received from Constantine ricocheted off his upper body to the boundary. A year later Larwood and Voce had been confined to the pages of history and leg theory abandoned, Constantine was warned for bowling Bodyline during the England tour of the Caribbean in 1934–35.

Aggression reared its head again with the raw and rapacious Fred Trueman who had the Indians diving for cover at his beloved Headingley in the first Test of the 1952 tour. Trueman blasted out three men with his first fourteen balls in the worst start to an innings in Test match history. The scoreboard read 0–4. Later in the same series he grabbed 8–31 which was the best haul by a paceman in Test matches. Unlike Statham, who was quiet and modest by nature, Trueman, his bowling partner for so many years, was raucous, wild and certainly not short on confidence.

'I always felt I was good enough to bowl at anyone. Always thought to myself, Fred, you can get this man out. The greater the player the more I relished the battle. Dennis Lillee had the same philosophy. He was averaging four and a half wickets a Test and they were costing him about 23 runs each so he knew that if he kept bowling, the wickets were bound to come. I used to glare at batsmen yes, that was part of it. So did George [Statham] but in a different way. He could be aggressive if he had to be. He was a great bowler – there's none any better than him. Never will be.'

Outstanding bowlers both of them, but bowlers of their time. Fast bowling, like everything else in life, has moved on. Line and length has an entirely different meaning if your name is Malcolm Marshall or Curtley Ambrose. It is no longer the case that each ball is designed to get the batsman out. Sophisticated brutalism, like it or not, is what confronts the Graham Gooches and Robin Smiths of this world when West Indies are in town.

Wes Hall and Charlie Griffith were the ogres in the 1960s, Griffith after he fired a ball at the Indian opening batsman Nari Contractor in 1961 which fractured the back of his skull. Contractor was gravely ill for hours on end, and although he recovered he never played international cricket again. Griffith at the time of writing was still playing club cricket in his native Barbados but refused to discuss his career. It seemed he was still sensitive about allegations that he threw his quicker ball – allegations which have become the popular explanation for a thunderbolt which materialized from nowhere and shocked the most seasoned batsmen.

Hall, while marginally less venomous because of a more orthodox action, was generally quicker than Griffith. His was the name with which fathers frightened their children. No one had previously witnessed such an explosion of speed. I remember first seeing him at Fenner's in 1966 when he drew gasps of amazement by placing his bowling mark beyond the boundary! We felt obliged to avert our gaze as he launched himself at the pale-faced undergraduate with a bat who was hoping to glimpse something red as it jetted through. There were not too many volunteers to open the England innings in those days. John Edrich was one of them. It was his misfortune to walk into the teeth of a gale. Not only did he have to score many of his Test runs against Hall, Griffith and Lillee and Thomson in their prime, but he caught the edge of the new Caribbean gust which started with Holding, Holder and Roberts. It is to his considerable credit that he managed more than 5,000 runs at an average of 43.54.

'We didn't play as many Test matches as they do now. They were more of an occasion. There were no one-day internationals when I started either, so you only had games at county level, apart from Tests. Although I had been on tour to India in 1961, it was nothing like the ordeal of going out to bat against the West Indies in 1963. With world-class players like Sobers, Kanhai and Worrell they had an air of confidence about them which was intimidating even before you got out to the wicket.

'What I remember most is the way the ball became a blur when Wes and Charlie bowled. They didn't always line it up too well to start with. They were a bit wild so you had a chance to acclimatize. I'd say they were about as fast as each other. The problem with Charlie was his suspect action. He would amble in at the same pace then let you have one which was three times quicker than anything else you'd seen. It was difficult to spot. The rocket ball was a yorker and nobody was going to have much of an answer to that. You always had the feeling that the umpires would call him any time, but they never did. In between he could drop down almost to medium pace.'

Griffith took 32 Test wickets on the 1963 tour as West Indies won the series 3–1. He took 119 overall, leaving a trail of physical destruction behind him. When the 'rocket ball' as Edrich calls it was not a yorker, it was an especially spiteful bouncer. Among those injured was John Hampshire who still feels the effects of being knocked out by a Griffith bouncer in a Yorkshire match at Middlesbrough.

It was during the Lord's Test that Cowdrey had his arm broken by Hall and found himself batting in the second innings with his arm in plaster as the game ended in a thrilling draw. Cowdrey remains sanguine about the episode.

'Wes was a true sportsman. He bowled good bouncers but there was no hint of malice about him. The broken arm was pure accident. It was a grey night at Lord's and there was no sightscreen at the pavilion end in those days. The ball took off very fast, I was late and it hit me on the forearm as I tried to punch it away from my throat. It was a bit like Graham Gooch in Trinidad. I put it in ice and water and then the pain started. Horrible. Funnily enough Roy Gilchrist, who was just as fast as Wes, hit me twice at Lord's on the 1957 tour and I still feel the pain in my hand thirty-four years later!

'It wasn't easy getting my mind in tune to make a comeback after the broken arm. I missed the rest of the season and remarkably the next ball I faced, on the Cavaliers tour of Jamaica, the bowler just happened to be Wes Hall. He realized half way through his run-up, stopped, said

"Gosh", and gave me a nice half-volley to get off the mark. That's the kind of chap he is.'

Edrich: 'Wes Hall was relatively easy to pick up in the same way that Lillee and Holding were because they had long flowing runs and you had an idea the ball was going to be in a certain area. That was never the case with Griffith, nor with Jeff Thomson who was the most difficult bowler I played against. His arm was behind his back before he let go so you had no idea where the ball was going. He also had the ability to get the ball up and over your head virtually off a length.

'On Mike Denness's tour of 1974 the problem wasn't so much bouncers. You can get out of the way of them. Tommo specialized in the chest ball. That takes a lot of playing. You have to give him credit. He was a very fine bowler. I remember Jim Laker sitting in the Noble Stand in Sydney watching Tommo's first three overs. He told us he'd never seen anyone bowl so quickly. He was white-faced with shock — and he didn't have to bat! Rod Marsh must have been at least thirty-five yards back and I think they only had one man in front of the wicket. We got 19 or 20 extras in those three overs and Marshy was getting furious. They were either flying over his head or thudding into his chest. We couldn't lay a bat on the ball.'

Thomson was a freak bowler, an old-fashioned slinger who could make the ball skid alarmingly. His exceptional speed meant that he was often able to escape punishment with bad balls and collect more than his fair share of wickets with full tosses and long-hops. He took 0–110 when he first appeared on the Test scene against Pakistan at Melbourne and was booed off the field. Gradually he learned more control. His greatest asset, as Edrich has explained, was getting the ball to snap at the batsman's rib-cage from just short of a length.

Lillee was much more of an artist, capable of moving the ball in the air and off the seam at great pace and possessing a slower ball almost as devastating as Lindwall's.

It might not sound like it listening to Edrich's description of the way Thomson was spraying the ball around the Sydney Cricket Ground, but fast bowling had undergone a further refinement. It started three years earlier with John Snow, who ruffled more Australian feathers than any English paceman since Larwood. Lillee was a better bowler after consulting Snow whom he had long admired. The important lesson was that intimidation alone was not enough. Instead of firing bouncers which were easily avoidable by good batsmen and therefore a waste of energy, better to target the area between hip and shoulder. Snow explains:

'That is the grey area, especially on overseas wickets where bounce is critical whether you're bowling pace or spin. You try to make the batsman play at something he thinks he can handle but finds he can't. I used to set the batsman up with a couple of deliveries of three-quarter pace then put something extra into the next one while making it look the same. That's the one you hope will be the wicket-taking ball which climbs to the hip and shoulder area. It's the most awkward delivery to handle and there's always a chance if he misses it of the batsman getting a blow in the ribs.'

Snow was supreme on Ray Illingworth's tour of 1970–71. His 31 wickets in the series were the most since Larwood's 32 in the Bodyline series and his aggressive bowling caused almost as big a stir. As early as the second Test in Perth he was warned by umpire Rowan for aiming three successive bouncers at Doug Walters. By the time of the deciding Test at Sydney it was like Adelaide 1933 all over again. Snow hit Jenner, the No. 10 batsman, with what the Australians called a bouncer. In fact the ball was travelling at chest height. Once more he was cautioned by Rowan, a signal for rioters in the crowd to pelt the field with beer cans. Illingworth led his team back to the pavilion before things eventually calmed down and England won by 62 runs to complete a splendid 2–0 series success. Illingworth had to rebuke Snow early on the tour but later the two became good friends.

'I defended John several times on that tour. It's pure rubbish to say I started the intimidation thing again by asking him to bowl bouncers. He wasn't bowling bouncers. After he'd been warned for supposedly bowling one bouncer he banged the next one in really short and it flew over the keeper's head. He turned to the umpire and said: "Now that's a bouncer!"

'If Snowy was going to hit you it wouldn't be above chest high. Jenner was on his hands and knees when he was hit. Intimidation is part of the game as long as you're not bowling to injure someone for the sake of it. Snowy had that great ability to drive a batsman on to the back foot shaping to play it through the covers, then beat him with extra lift and movement. You can't take that away from anyone. Ambrose can bounce it chest high all day because of his height. So could Garner and occasionally Lillee. Bouncers were no use to them. If you took out of the game the element of intimidation John Snow specialized in, you might as well stop playing. You'd turn someone with outstanding ability into an average performer.'

A one-off, was Snow. Invariably drifting into a world of his own. A world of poetry – he had three anthologies published – where the more tiresome aspects of Test and county cricket would be an irritating intrusion. This is an extract from one of the poems of which he is proudest called 'Lord's Test'.

> Later, spiritlike,
> while Father Time above the northern stand eyes the breeze,
> you move aside
> and see a body flailing,
> bowl a ball swinging
> along its way, batsman playing
> and remember, outside the wall
> people weave their webs of life
> with you on the lattice day
> which is everyone's,
> yet is an age within an age
> a life within a life,
> as minutes pass awestruck
> up to lunch and over

The selectors once dropped him for one Test after a lethargic performance at Old Trafford in 1969 when Illingworth enforced the follow-on against West Indies, much to Snow's annoyance. In Adelaide in 1971, he was on autopilot in a warm-up match against South Australia, 'lollypopping' around the boundary as Illingworth describes it, while Peter Lever and Ken Shuttleworth, the bowlers, were getting more and more incensed. The captain ordered his main strike bowler to report to his hotel room at 8 p.m. sharp. This was the lecture:

'Snowy, I'm treating you as an intelligent person. If you weren't you'd be on the boat home. You're buggering about in the field. If you continue I shall have no bowlers who want to bowl. As regards your bowling, I can't understand your thinking sometimes. You watch a tailender whack the ball back over your head without appearing to care, whereas Fred Trueman would say, "Give me that ball and I'll pin 'im to the sightscreen!" I know you've a different mentality and it doesn't affect you the same way, but you're going to have to bowl a bit faster to get your rhythm right for the Tests. You can't just turn it on and off like a tap. And one thing you must do is give me 100 per cent in the field. If you don't it's finished. I don't care if I lose the series – I'll do it without you if I have to.'

Illingworth believes that years of misuse by Sussex were to blame for Snow's occasional 'dropouts'. Because they had a world-class bowler there was a temptation to bowl him for twenty overs a day on wickets which offered nothing. 'They didn't get the best out of him because he got his back up. As soon as Snowy gets his back up you've lost him.'

He was vociferous about players' rights during the latter part of his career, particularly the poor rewards on offer for Test cricketers who worked hard to keep in top condition, attracted big audiences and were paid peanuts. Naturally this did not endear him to TCCB officials in whose eyes he was always a firebrand. A thinking cricketer, though, with a deep love of the game. He attached great importance to the psychology of successful fast bowling.

'The majority of Test players have reached a certain standard of ability, so the deciding factor has to be how that ability is best employed. You have to set about achieving superiority over your opponents. That's where the mental side comes in. That's why it's so important to sow that seed of doubt in the batsman's mind while you are sparring at the start of a match. You have to work out his weakness, make him feel inferior. It's an individual contest within a team game. Once you've established that psychological edge – which needs the support of the fielders too – all sorts of mistakes are possible. The batsman can see ghosts which might not be there. That is what makes cricket such a great game.

'Although you have to be a masochist to enjoy bowling fast, it's a fabulous feeling when everything's running smoothly. The ultimate thrill is the knowledge that pace bowling is the only type of bowling which has repeatedly changed the course of the game. Speed defeats reactions.'

The game turned uglier when Denness led England back to Australia in 1974–75. Not only did Ian Chappell have Lillee at his best, Thomson at his wildest and Max Walker at his most efficient, but England had decided to leave Snow at home and Geoff Boycott backed out of the limelight, to be accused of varying degrees of cowardice. His opening partner Edrich was upset by what he saw and heard.

'The attitude of the entire Australian side was very aggressive. You expect a tough time but there was malice in the air. Chappell was building a new team and wanted to show his home supporters how far they'd come since England were last there. There was absolutely no pleasure in it. The younger players were all subject to abuse and many of them were intimidated by it. The Australian team's behaviour encouraged the crowd to turn hostile. Every time Lillee or Thomson came in to bowl, there'd be loud chants of "Kill, kill, kill!" I'd never experienced anything quite like it.

'The nearest was in the West Indies when we won in 1968. There were riots in Jamaica and some very fast bowling coming our way. The difference was that we had strength and experience in the side. Kenny

Barrington wouldn't give in to it, nor would Tom Graveney or Colin Cowdrey. Australia was a very unhappy time for most of us. I got a couple of broken ribs from Lillee in Sydney and Dennis Amiss fractured his thumb.'

A fractured thumb was the least of Amiss's worries. He came home from that long and arduous tour utterly disillusioned with cricket, devoid of confidence and convinced there was something drastically wrong with the technique he had employed throughout his career. You cannot get much lower. Dennis had fulfilled an ambition by touring Australia. Nevertheless he began to sense that his points of reference were strangely unfamiliar. The clues he would expect to pick up were being missed. This was his first miscalculation.

'Of the three pace bowlers, I came to the conclusion Max Walker was the danger man. I thought Lillee had lost some of his sting after his back problems and as for Thomson, frankly I didn't think he'd be chosen. How wrong can you be? Thomson hit me in the Adam's apple with the first ball of our match against Queensland. It hurt a lot. I shudder now when I think about it.

'When Brian Luckhurst and I came to bat in the first Test, I realized I'd also underestimated Lillee. He was bowling much faster than he had in the warm-up games. He also made the ball lift and leave the bat disconcertingly. Even at that early stage I had the feeling he was going to be a nightmare.

'I shall never forget the fourth evening of that Test when Brian and I had an hour to negotiate until the close of play. It was the most awe-inspiring spell of fast bowling I'd ever faced. Lillee and Thomson bowled like men possessed on a rough Brisbane wicket. Not bouncers – worse than that. Both were pitching the ball just short of a length but you had no clue how high it would bounce at you. Thomson was warned for sending three whistling past my chin in failing light. He didn't take a blind bit of notice and made no attempt to pitch the ball up – if anything the next four flew even faster past my face. To my relief we went off because of bad light. We lost the match heavily although Tony Greig scored a defiant hundred in his own improvised way. I had a sleepless night before discovering that my thumb was broken. I had been clobbered by both bowlers. My morale was starting to go.'

The same applied to the rest of the England party, from Denness who had neither the credentials as a batsman or as captain to counteract this furious onslaught, to John Edrich, his much more experienced and battle-hardened vice-captain, who needed pain-killing injections in his hand. The exceptions were Alan Knott and Greig who seemed to derive a vicarious pleasure from 'going in where it hurts' as footballers might say. We shall take a closer look at the man destined to take over the captaincy in the next chapter. In the meantime, with Edrich, David Lloyd and Amiss crocked, the selectors sent for Colin Cowdrey. Answering the call in the depths of an England winter, where he planned to celebrate his forty-second Christmas, Cowdrey did well. He was the first to hook Thomson. It was beyond the bounds of reason that he could single-handedly raise the spirits of a shell-shocked squad.

Edrich had already complained about an excess of aggression. For the first time since Larwood, who refused to apologize for his actions and was banished from Test cricket as a result, here were a couple of pacemen who displayed no remorse for the fear they instilled nor the damage they caused. Lillee in his autobiography declared brazenly:

'I try to hit a batsman in the rib-cage when I bowl a purposeful bouncer. I want it to hurt so much that the batsman doesn't want to face me any more. I want to be in complete control in the situation and that's one way of keeping hold of the reins.'

Lillee claimed that he was only expressing what every fast bowler thought and felt but was too ashamed to admit. He has to be admired for his frankness if not his bloodthirsty instincts. The surprising thing is that he had recovered from four stress fractures of the spine to take part in that series. Even the most optimistic commentators did not believe he could become completely rehabilitated, but they reckoned without his smouldering desire to get back at the world's leading batsmen. He spent six weeks in a plaster cast, felt his way back over the previous year and declared himself fully fit by the time Denness's Jumbo jet touched down. He took 24 wickets in the first five Tests and inflicted on the demoralized Amiss his third consecutive Test duck in the sixth at Melbourne. Lillee was, in every sense, the rampaging warrior, aquiline features, Zapata moustache bristling, crucifix flying around his neck as he raced in to bowl. The verbal exchanges with the England batsmen were caustic, his rapport with the Australian crowds that of the toreador who holds aloft the ear of the tortured bull as a mark of his machismo. Amiss and others were reduced to a mental shambles.

'Several times I walked to the middle beaten before I started. The bat in my hand seemed superfluous against those two. With no helmets, and no chest protection until Cowdrey showed us how to do it, batting was a complete misery.'

Bernie Thomas, the England physiotherapist and trainer, made the players a suit of foam-rubber 'armour' like the equipment Cowdrey had brought with him. It was worn across the chest and down whichever side of the rib-cage was nearer the bowler. The makeshift paraphernalia was held in position around the neck with a strip of elastic. Amiss opened the innings in the fourth Test at Sydney fortified by his corporeal protection if nothing else.

'The first ball of the innings from Lillee was an enormous bouncer which flew over Marsh's head and hit the sightscreen one bounce. I thought: "Shit! We've got a contest here." It was a lethal wicket. I kept telling myself: "Come on Dennis, fight it out!"

'I was fending and ducking but managed to get to 30 playing my best innings of the series. Suddenly I was out caught Marsh bowled Lillee *again*! It pitched off-stump. I had to play it. It bounced and left me. Why did I keep getting unbelievable deliveries from Lillee? He used to say: "Amiss? I could bowl him out with an orange!" He had such an edge over me I was ready to give up the game.

'People were telling me I had to change my technique. Boycott's words kept coming back. He said I'd never be a Test batsman playing off the front foot. I got bogged down with theory instead of sticking to my own way of playing. The newspapers had a go at me. I found it difficult to look people in the eye when I came back. Some players smiled and said: "They're great bowlers," but it got to me personally.'

There was no escape for Denness's ravaged troops. Australia were due in England in a few months' time by which time major surgery, not to say psychiatry, would be *de rigeur* if similar horrors were not to be revisited. How England faced up to that when they had to all intents and purposes exhausted the supply of competent batsmen we shall see. Needless to say when the body is weak, the mind has to be strong.

Lillee was the brains behind the Australian pace attack, Thomson was the slugger. A fiery youngster originally from Sydney who did not take kindly to interference from authority, he was banned for life from local football when he broke a referee's nose because he disagreed with a free-kick decision. In a magazine article published a few months before the England tour he was quoted as saying, 'I enjoy hitting a batsman more than getting him out. It doesn't worry me in the least to see a batsman hurt, rolling around screaming and blood on the pitch.' He dismissed those quotes as 'garbage' but when I spoke to him at the Gabba where he is manager/coach to the Queensland team, it was obvious that the author only required a little poetic licence to stray into the 'garbage' area. Thomson still has no regard for batsmen.

'There was nothing I wanted to do as a kid but bowl as fast as possible. The other kids at school were terrified of me. I bowled like my Dad. Catapult action. Like a Greg Norman golf swing using the full arc. It took nothing out of my body. It was so easy for me. I can still bowl at 80 miles an hour today. Not many people can say that at forty-one.

'The most important thing is to get the upper hand straight away. Let the batsman know you don't like 'im. It's a mind game but I didn't need any psyching up. I detested the bloke at the other end and I hated it when anyone scored a run off me in front of the wicket. It was lovely when it smacked into the keeper's gloves.'

It was a fact that Jeff could be more dangerous in his second spell than his first. When the ball was new it was difficult for him to control.

'I could bowl line and length if I wanted. No fun in that. All Dennis and I wanted to do was blast the shit out of the Englishmen. As long as it hit the seam and went past 'em at 100 miles an hour that's all I bothered. If someone got hit, tough. You don't drive racing cars if you're frightened of crashing.

'Having said that, my greatest thrill as a youngster was to smash the ball into the stumps. Knock a stump out of the ground. Break the bails if I could or send 'em as far back as possible. Bouncers flying a mile over the batsman's head were a total waste of time. Dennis and I worked that out pretty early.'

FOUR
The Fourth Dimension

'They are giants, and if you are afraid, go away and say your
prayers, whilst I advance and engage them in fierce and
unequal battle.'

DON QUIXOTE (Cervantes)

With a single grenade at your disposal you can blast anyone to
smithereens on your day. Pakistan were twice the team because of
Imran Khan, as were India with Kapil Dev and New Zealand with
Richard Hadlee. When you have two high explosives to hand, few
sides can live with you. Most of the best fast bowlers hunted in pairs:
Larwood and Voce; Trueman and Statham; Lindwall and Miller;
Lillee and Thomson. Should you be fortunate enough to come across a
whole boxful of fire-crackers, you are close to omnipotence. No-one
had dreamed of pace men hunting in packs of four until Clive Lloyd
ushered Test Cricket into a new dimension from which its head is still
spinning.

The best batsman in the world has only a 50–50 chance of surviving
the new ball when he faces Lillee or Marshall on a wicket with pace
and bounce. In Geoff Boycott's case, the man delivering the most
unplayable over he ever faced was Michael Holding, although it could
have been any one of four titanic pace men waiting their turn. The year
was 1981, the venue Bridgetown, Barbados. Boycott was barbecued
and eaten alive during what was surely one of the hottest opening
overs in Test history.

The atmosphere in the Kensington Oval was seismic that Saturday.
The Barbados government had decided to ignore Guyana's political
stance over Robin Jackman and proceed with the tour. It might have
been better, with hindsight, if it had called the whole thing off. West
Indies scored 265 and Clive Lloyd opened the bowling with Andy
Roberts downwind. Holding would bowl a short spell into the breeze
from the pavilion end before switching to relieve Roberts. He felt
good.

'I was warm and loose coming out of the dressing-room. No worries about getting into a rhythm. I felt so good I just ran in and bowled flat out. At twenty-seven years of age you can do that. I can't honestly say I knew something was going to happen but it was very quick for an opening over.'

The first ball took Boycott on the glove but fell short of the slips; the second he played at and missed; the third nipped back and caught him on the thigh; the fourth and fifth were played down uneasily in front of gully and the last ball ripped out a stump. Boycott, who had looked by far the most solid of the England batsmen while making 70 in the previous Test in Trinidad, now looked a novice. He was seldom clean bowled. Sections of the crowd danced on the tin roof of the stand. You knew that if Boycott could not handle it, no one else was likely to. The memory of Holding's sixth ball is vivid.

'It went like a rifle bullet and I may just have played a fraction inside it, expecting him to pitch up. Six good reasons why I never advise anyone to become a Test opening batsman! . . . better to be a mid-order batsman and come in when the ball is old and there is a chance the spinners will be on.'

Fast bowlers grow tired relatively soon. That is their weakness. Given the right amount of watchfulness and good fortune it is possible to blunt the most furious opening salvo – provided the wicket is less helpful than Bridgetown. The picture changes when, instead of spinners or medium-pacers, the opening pair are relieved by two more bowlers of similar pace and equal spite. Then it is no more comfortable to be the mid-order batsman Boycott envies than the man taking the first blows. Neither does the opener who weathers the storm have any shelter to look forward to. Lloyd conceived the ultimate trap. Morning, noon and night the batsman was under siege.

Roberts, Holding, Croft and Garner. The world's first genuine all-pace attack. Garner was not as rapid as the others most of the time. He was expert at playing the dentist's drill on an exposed nerve and likely to send you through the roof with the occasional throat-high express. Boycott summed up the dilemma.

'The ace in their pack of quick bowlers is Joel Garner. If they feel they are running into trouble, West Indies can always bring on giant Joel and there is no way you can get after him – nobody ever has. So one end is sealed as far as free scoring is concerned. Batsmen feel they are under pressure, and it only needs one of the three faster men to come off. It may be Croft one day, Holding the next, Roberts another . . . whichever way you are in trouble.'

Lloyd's unwavering faith in the power of speed wherever the match, whatever the conditions, was answered by a veritable production line of young hopefuls from every island under the sun. Trinidad, hardly a hotbed of hostility, in the playing sense at any rate, produced Ian Bishop who, until his back injury, was the most slippery of the lot. When England resolved to go down the same route – with some success – on the West Indies tour of 1989–90, two of their most successful front-line bowlers, Devon Malcolm and Gladstone Small, were of Caribbean origin. Three more of the same origin, Philip DeFreitas, David Lawrence and Chris Lewis, were let loose on Viv Richards's visiting West Indies in the summer of 1991. Indeed, since the retirement from Test cricket of Fred Trueman in 1965, only two Englishmen with white skin have emerged as world-class fast bowlers – John Snow and Bob Willis.

Only in exceptional circumstances would the opposition have the time or the talent to score 300 against Roberts, Holding, Croft and Garner, the foursome Lloyd still regards as the best.

'I don't see how you could improve on that. Andy was the quiet assassin. Much quicker than he seemed. He could make the old ball climb off a length. Michael we christened "Whispering Death" because he skipped over the ground so lightly that you couldn't hear him coming. A 400-metre record holder at school. Joel we called "Mr Mean". He could put it right there all day. You knew for sure you weren't going to see too many runs scored. His yorker was as shattering as Charlie Griffith's. Colin Croft was the most warlike. He wouldn't mess about. Took his cricket very seriously.'

Aside from Holding's opening over to Boycott at Bridgetown, it was Croft who dominated the four-match series of 1981. He took 24 wickets – more than anyone else – and exuded such an air of foreboding that the contest became distinctly sinister. The abiding image is of the big Guyanese raising clouds of dust as his boot scraped the baked earth before he began his run-up. What an approach it was, too. Croft ran so wide of the crease at the point of delivery that the ball would appear out of the crowd at a ground like Antigua where the sightscreen is a whitewashed wall. You cannot move a wall. Boycott has this to say:

'You want to get forward and across to him, but Croft's nobody's fool. Every so often he lets you have one in the ribs to keep you back and at 6 ft 4 in he's not the slowest bowler in Test cricket. I suppose it would be possible to get forward to every delivery – and play him with your helmet.

'Croft gives the lie to so many accepted rules for successful fast bowling. "Deliver the ball from close to the stumps with a side-on action," they say. Well, Croft's feet are all over the place, his left foot is outside the return crease, his arms wave like windmills and his chest is square as he lets the ball go. A hundred Test wickets with that action? Try explaining that to youngsters in the nets.'

It was an ugly tour for several reasons, not least of which was the débâcle in Guyana. England were mightily relieved to escape from Georgetown, none more so than Ken Barrington who was concerned about the team's safety. The thought of armed troops along the route to the airport as players and reporters hurried to catch an unscheduled flight filled Kenny with alarm. The tension may well have contributed to his untimely and fatal heart attack after the party reached the sanctuary of Bridgetown. He was also profoundly worried about the West Indian pacemen. The nightmare of Hall and Griffith at their most lethal had returned in double vision. As much as any batsman in modern times Barrington knew about the psychological 'wall' a batsman had to climb to survive. Many times he stressed to the players on that tour the importance of staying at the wicket, trying to eliminate any possible error, waiting and watching and reminding yourself that bowlers get weary just as batsmen do. Sound advice from someone who was dropped for scoring too slowly when making 258 against Australia. How England could have done with him now.

Barrington though never had to face anything like this. Four fast men coming at you the whole time on wickets designed to help them. On the morning of the second day of the third Test he accidentally caught Graham Gooch a nasty blow on the finger while bowling his leg-spinners in the nets. It was not bad enough to affect Gooch's performance in the match but Bernie Thomas had a tough job consoling Kenny.

'I told him not to upset himself so. No one injures a member of his own team on purpose. Kenny got himself into an awful state. Coming on top of the trouble in Guyana, it was too much for him. We should perhaps have seen the danger signs.'

Holding's over to Boycott later that day was the prelude to a painful England collapse. On a wicket condemned by Boycott as 'disgraceful', they were shot out for 122, their lowest total in a Barbados Test, and invited to follow on. Holding had taken 3–16, Croft 4–39. Barrington watched it all with increasing discomfort. He thought the cricket was vicious although, as luck would have it, no one was hit. His former Surrey team-mate, John Edrich, was with him that evening minutes before he died.

'He took on everyone's problems, Kenny. He was terrific at advising and coaching people but he couldn't just leave it there. When those chaps went out there to bat he went with them. What happened in the middle affected him very badly. I went to have dinner with him in the evening. Afterwards he said: "See you tomorrow. Come and have a net with us." That was the last time I saw him.

'Kenny was a lovely fellow and such a fine cricketer but I've never seen anyone get so nervous before a match. He seemed unable to relax. I shared a room with him on three tours and he was always up at six o'clock in the morning for a cup of tea and a cigarette. Sometimes earlier on Test match days.

'The West Indies thing got to him, especially on the 1968 tour. He'd written articles in a national newspaper accusing Charlie Griffith of throwing, and the crowd started to pick on him. They chanted: "Charlie's going to get you, Charlie's going to get you!" It built up into a big thing in Kenny's mind.'

His Test career had been curtailed at the age of thirty-eight when he suffered a heart attack during a double-wicket competition in Melbourne. The stress and worry of the days leading up to that Black Saturday in Bridgetown were the last things he needed.

One player very badly affected by the tour was Brian Rose, Botham's Somerset colleague, who did not get beyond the first Test. Rose had an awful time as a left-hander trying to counteract Croft and company on a moderately-paced Port of Spain track. He had struggled to find a semblance of form in the island games and never seemed likely to come to terms with Test cricket in the Caribbean. Having battled for an hour for ten runs in the first innings, Rose was a shambling, disconsolate figure when England followed-on and he found himself back at the crease in the No. 3 position with only 19 runs on the board. This time his agony was short-lived. Pushing at a full-length ball from Holding, he got a faint edge and was taken by Deryck Murray behind the wicket. That was the end of Rose's Test career. He spent a week or so dodging torrential rain and getting devoured by mosquitoes in Guyana before discovering he had eye problems and returning home.

'I played four Tests against the West Indies, three at home and one in Trinidad and throughout that time I faced only one over from Viv Richards. The rest was from four of the most ferocious and intimidating fast men on earth. They were after your blood. The subsequent crop aren't as hostile as Roberts, Holding, Garner and Croft. I doubt whether anyone could be. You had to dominate your own fear before you could go out there.

'The most dangerous physically was Croft because he bowled across the left-hander. If you went the correct way from leg to off to get behind the ball, it followed you. He was so tall that the ball always came chest high. If you didn't hook it was very hard to get away. Andy was a very clever bloke at bowling bouncers. He'd set you up with a slow one to make you think things weren't so bad after all, then he'd let you have a terrifyingly quick one. He set Derek Randall up that way in a county match. Derek hooked the first. The next one took his helmet off and he was very lucky not to be in hospital.

'My problem was that I couldn't see clearly out of my leading eye, the right. Anything pitched outside leg-stump was hard to pick up. I came home thinking I'd never play again.'

He did though, but only on an occasional basis for Somerset over the next three years.

As formidable as that quartet was, it was not until the mid-1980s and the emergence of Malcolm Marshall that batting against the West Indies carried a health warning as well as the normal risk of humiliating defeat. Croft had disappeared from the scene when Lloyd brought his men to England in 1984 for the first of two 'blackwash' series which finished David Gower's unhappy period in charge. Holding, Garner and Marshall were now supported by Eldine Baptiste and Winston Davis, a combination which brushed England aside with contemptuous ease, and sent two young batsmen to hospital.

Andy Lloyd had waited a long time for his England chance. It came that summer, when he was twenty-eight years old. It lasted thirty-two minutes. On his home patch at Edgbaston the Warwickshire opener was struck an almighty blow by a short, skidding ball from Marshall which crashed into the side of his head.

'It was the first ball of the seventh over. I thought it was passing over my shoulder but it kept low. I realized it was going to hit me straight between the eyes so I tried to corkscrew out of the way. It caught me right next to the eye. I *saw* it hit me. Desmond Haynes and Clive Lloyd came to help but I don't remember hearing anything from Malcolm. I went down. I couldn't see much out of my right eye. Then Bernie Thomas told me I had to go off. Some of the cones and rods behind the retina which transmit signals to the brain had been destroyed. The majority have regenerated but I still have a blind spot in the right eye.'

Lloyd never played Test cricket again. Nor after that series did Paul Terry, the young Hampshire batsman who had a forearm broken by Davis in the fourth Test. Terry came back at the end of the innings with his arm in a sling. West Indies won both matches at a canter. Fear as well as inability to play the fast rising ball had taken a murderous grip. For the best part of a decade until England won their first Test in the Caribbean for twenty-two years on Gooch's tour of 1989–90, West Indies pacemen did more or less as they chose. Even with one arm!

The arch slayer, Marshall, damaged himself in the third Test at Headingley, diving in the gully to stop a shot from Chris Broad. The news that the world's most feared express might be out of the match within an hour of the start was music to the ears of the England team, as Broad recalled.

'. . . it was not so much a question of sighs of relief in the dressing-room – more genuine celebration . . . we thought the West Indies, being a bowler short, would not be able to keep up the pressure with the never-ending pace barrage that had beaten us in the past.'

He could not have been wider of the mark. There is nothing more dangerous than a wounded tiger. Not only did Marshall bat one-handed to enable West Indies to secure a first-innings lead, but he rendered them speechless ten minutes later by taking the new ball with a bandaged arm. He blasted out Broad, somehow caught and bowled Graeme Fowler and then trapped the first-innings hero and centurion, Allan Lamb, lbw for 3. After the rest day he reduced his pace for maximum swing and movement to end the match with a career-best 7–53.

Marshall has injured more batsmen than anyone in Test cricket, probably because his speed is deceptive and he's not particularly tall. He generates pace with the whippiness of his arm at the moment of release, rather like Mike Procter, who insists he did not bowl off the wrong foot but fooled us into thinking so because his arm moved faster than his legs. Come 1986 England were desperate for a chink of light down the long black tunnel. There would be no respite. Patrick Patterson, a muscular Jamaican with a bustling action and a horizontal left leg, was the latest piece in the jigsaw, with Holding, Marshall and Garner still firing on all cylinders.

Before the tour was very old, Marshall had consigned one of England's leading batsmen to hospital. It was another fearful blow. Mike Gatting performed well in the early part of the tour, spending a lot of time at the wicket, programming his mind for the enormous task ahead. Then came the one-day international in Jamaica.

'The wicket was slightly undulating. Not pleasant. Patterson was on one end and Macko [Marshall] the other. I'd gone in No. 3. The first two from Malcolm I let go by my chest. Then I played one down in front of me, trying to get the pace of the wicket. The next ball was fairly short and flew – I think I started going forward and ended up going back as it got big on me. Eventually I tried to get out of the way but it came over the top of the bat. I felt as though I'd been hit by a brick. Something pushed my face inwards then stopped suddenly. I knew I'd broken my nose again. I didn't go down but I did stumble and knock a bail off.

'I felt dazed but not too bad. I wanted to go out again but they told me I couldn't because I was out. Ian Botham came to the hospital with me. The worst bit was when the guy put five or six stitches in my face.

'The blood was seeping down my throat. They'd packed my nose with wadding so I could hardly breathe and I had to sit upright in bed while I tried to sleep. I woke up choking a couple of times. It was like coming up for air in a swimming pool. Awful feeling.

'At the time Malcolm said nothing. He went to pick up the ball and dropped it sharpish when he found half an inch of bone in it. He came to the hotel to see how I was a couple of days later and I said not to worry – it was my fault, or the wicket's.

'There was no point letting fear or apprehension hold me back after I returned. Macko didn't make it easy for me but I didn't expect him to. There's a lot of adrenalin pumping round your system when you start playing again. You wonder how you'll react to the first ball. I managed to hang around. I've been to Australia since although perhaps I've not batted quite so well as before.'

As you would expect from such a pugnacious character, Gatting defends Marshall's, or any other fast bowler's, right to use the short-pitched ball, no doubt in the knowledge that he would encourage similar tactics if he had a bowler of similar calibre in his own ranks. Andy Lloyd is equally magnanimous.

'If a batsman is scared of the ball he shouldn't be in this job. I was just unlucky to reach my best form when the West Indies were here. The bouncer is an essential part of a fast bowler's armoury and should never be banned. It's an exciting part of cricket. West Indies cricket is based on self-belief. Not many of them wear helmets, so why should we complain?'

Both agree that Marshall is a charming bloke off the field. There are few who would dispute that. In his adopted county, Hampshire, he is a popular figure at social functions, where they appreciate his contribution to the cricket club while barely recognizing the mean machine who chews up batsmen and spits them out. Marshall's county captain, Mark Nicholas, finds him a fascinating study.

'He's a lovely man with a deep and honourable love of the game.

Yes, he's hit more players than anyone but his view is that the ball does the hitting, not him. He's a fast bowler, they've got a bat. End of subject.

'Along with Hadlee he's the greatest bowler of the 1980s. Andy Roberts was as good but not as motivated. Between them Marshall and Roberts have changed cricket completely in the last ten years: the decade of the assassin with blinding pace. Malcolm can bowl everything from inswing and outswing and cutters to lightning speed at your head. He only intimidates people when he knows they have a weakness for it. Many batsmen are beaten before they take guard. Dilip Vengsarkar for one. Malcolm regards him as fodder. He even got Vengsarkar caught at gully in the Bicentenary Test on the flattest Lord's wicket you could imagine.'

Marshall also has an infuriating (if you are a batsman) knack of nominating his dismissals. When Hampshire were playing Berkshire in one of the Benson & Hedges group matches, Nicholas did not plan to use him much. It seemed a trifle extravagant against an unsuspecting Minor Counties side. Marshall persuaded his captain to give him a couple of overs at Grahame Roope, the former Surrey and England No. 3 who might have been a stumbling block. 'I'll trap him leg before then you can get on with the rest of the game,' he promised. Three balls later Roope was out, lbw Marshall. His bravado did not always bear fruit but there were other occasions when it did, as Nicholas told me.

'He once nominated Clive Radley and Phil Edmonds when we played Middlesex. Sure enough they were dismissed in quick succession. The most memorable occasion was against Leicestershire in a Sunday League game in 1989. Malcolm had just come back from a series in the West Indies and was warming up on a pitch alongside the match wicket. Chris Lewis was the batsman waiting to receive. Malcolm said: "Look at these, skipper," and I replied: "Yes, outswingers, good." "No," he repeated, "have a good look." I told him I didn't follow his drift. Then he explained: "I'm bowling outswingers to fool Lewis who's watching me. In a minute I'll let him have an inswinger which'll remove his off-stump." It happened exactly as he predicted.

'I honestly don't know how people coped with him in 1982 when he took 132 championship wickets. The player I think who consistently handles him without too much bother is Mark Benson of Kent. My only criticism of Malcolm is that he hasn't bowled enough at the stumps. Benson has worked that out. He leaves a lot of deliveries.'

Nicholas, who once captained the England 'B' team on tour and has had a closer view than most of Roberts and Marshall in day-to-day action, has interesting views on the changing face of fast bowling where attention has switched away from the stumps back towards the body.

'Brian Statham was a great bowler but the thinking has changed. That business about only bowling at the wicket because that is all that matters is folklore rubbish. Colin Cowdrey and Peter May never had to fend off chest-high balls all day. Given the choice, most batsmen would sooner face Statham or Trueman than Malcolm Marshall.'

He is almost certainly right, although on a favourable wicket it is open to speculation which of the three would claim the most victims.

The thread throughout the West Indies' 'Reign of Terror' at its height was Holding, a softly spoken and mild-mannered Jamaican whose strict family background was an unlikely apprenticeship for a bogeyman. Here is a peep into the mind of a West Indian fast bowler. It should raise a few eyebrows and dispel a few myths.

'The happy-go-lucky spirit didn't exist in the early days of my career. It was war. Talking to opposing batsmen or fielders was out of the question, unless I cracked a sarcastic joke. I once hit Bruce Laird [Australian Test batsman] in the box then asked him if he had any kids. "Yes, two," he said. "Good," I replied, "you won't be needing any more, then!" It wasn't until I got older and more mature that I became friendly with the opposition. You gradually realize they're only human beings like you, out to make a living.

'If you're a fast bowler you can't be thinking, "I won't bowl like that because the batsman might get hurt"! It puts too much pressure on you and ruins your style. You just have to do the job you've been chosen to do because the batsman's doing the same. You hope no one gets hurt. I don't like to see that. In the latter part of my career I started to think thoughts I didn't have when I was twenty-two, such as "This fellah's got a wife and family!" It didn't change the way I bowled. I hoped the next time he'd get a glove on it instead of getting his head in the way.

'I'd assume that was also true of Malcolm. Colin Croft was more aggressive. He liked playing the tough guy but a lot of it was talk. Colin was mean but I doubt that he could hit someone and honestly say he enjoyed it. He always said he had no regrets. That's slightly different from getting pleasure out of seeing blood. I disagreed with Colin on one matter. If he hit someone he'd stare at them. That was wrong. The first thing you do is go and help and make sure he's okay. There's no point standing on your mark staring.

'Andy Roberts is a very different person. He was a tremendous help when I got into Test cricket. That was all down to Clive Lloyd. I didn't think I was good enough to get into the West Indies team. I was a lot quicker than Keith Boyce, Vanburn Holder and Bernard Julien but nowhere near in the same class. Clive voted for me on the Australian tour after the World Cup in 1975. At that stage Andy was the bowler I most admired. He was quicker than me but he didn't bowl at full speed throughout a spell. He'd bowl an express delivery or an express over now and then. When I bowled, every ball was the same speed.

'On the Australian tour I only took ten wickets in five Tests. If I'd been English that would have been it for me. The first Test was dreadful. My figures were 0–100-plus. After a while I began to room with Andy. That's when I started to learn all about fast bowling. Our discussions would go long into the evening. Thanks to him I got my first Test wicket. Max Walker was batting nine or ten. Andy came over and said: "Just bang one in short outside the off-stump." I told him I was tired. I didn't think I could get one to bounce high just then. He wouldn't take no for an answer. I ran up and did exactly what Andy had told me. Walker fended at it and was caught in the slips.

'Andy was very wise. Not many people liked him because he seemed aloof and unapproachable. He much preferred to sit in a corner on his own. If someone tried to talk to him when he wasn't in the mood he'd walk away and leave them. That's the way he was. Not deliberately stand-offish, but shy. He used to sit me down to analyse the behaviour of batsmen. He'd say, "What did you notice about that particular batsman and the way he reacted to you? It's important to study their little movements before and after the ball's delivered." These were things I wouldn't have noticed until he drew my attention to them. Learning to pick up the vibes, to notice little signs of fear by studying the batsman's eyes and learning to read his mind. Not by glaring, just looking and observing. Even after a good shot – perhaps a cut or a straight drive for 4 – it was important to watch the batsman's face. Was he really pleased with himself or was he worried that he might have annoyed you so much that the next one would rear up at him? All those signals you could detect in a batsman's face. It was part of the psychological duel.' Bernie Thomas tried to fathom Andy Roberts but failed. 'He spent a lot of his time reading comics and cartoons. He saw people firing guns in his cartoons and I guess he just transferred that to real life when he bowled. He got no more pleasure out of one than the other. An odd bloke.'

Holding continues, 'Although the four-man pace attack was winning us most of our games, I still got very nervous before a Test day. Some of the others were relaxed enough to go down town shopping. I couldn't do that. I'd practise on the morning before a Test then go to my room, lie down and watch television. I get no relaxation out of alcohol. In fact I don't like it because it stops me being in control. The first time I ever drank beer was in Pakistan in 1981. Dennis Waight, our coach, got some bottles from the High Commission one day when we were bored. He kept saying, "Go on Michael, there's nothing wrong with one bottle a day." People who think we lead a glamorous life on tour might be surprised to hear that.

'I was brought up very strictly. No drugs, nothing. I wasn't even allowed to drink *tea* when I was young because of the caffeine. My mother wouldn't have a celebration drink on her eightieth birthday. She's a Christian and so am I. Prayer is important to me – not that I pray for seven wickets or anything so specific. If it was that simple everyone would be praying for things they want and we'd all be happy for the rest of our lives. Very often I've had the feeling that I'm getting outside help. Some people call it a sixth sense. I believe it's something that's been put there by someone.'

If Holding's first tour of Australia was indifferent, his performances in England the following summer were positively volcanic. The touchpaper was lit by England's extravagant 1976 captain, Tony Greig, with his promise to 'make the West Indians grovel'. The remark was as subtle as an air raid; the English batsmen were duly shelled from all sides. Old Trafford was the first graveyard. Lloyd's men won by 425 runs, Holding, Roberts and Daniel filling Greig with dread.

'Two of the bravest batsmen we ever had were reduced to nervous wrecks by the most dangerous short-pitched bowling I've ever witnessed. The wicket was completely unsuitable for a Test match to begin with and I shall never forgive the authorities for allowing it. How John Edrich and Brian Close survived that evening session without losing their wickets and their lives I shall never know. When my turn came, it was the first time in my career I felt frightened. For two pence I'd have given the game up there and then. I felt as though my world had collapsed. The quick men had got to me.'

Lloyd was not entirely happy, though. 'We received a lot of carping criticism when Holding and Daniel bowled them a succession of bouncers late one afternoon, but it was up to the umpires to call the bowling intimidatory if they saw fit. It wasn't my duty to intervene. I wasn't pleased with the bowling because Close and Edrich were still there. Bouncers were no good for getting wickets. I told the quicks to bowl a fuller length and use the bouncer as a surprise.'

For the record, England, with Close (aged forty-five) forced to open

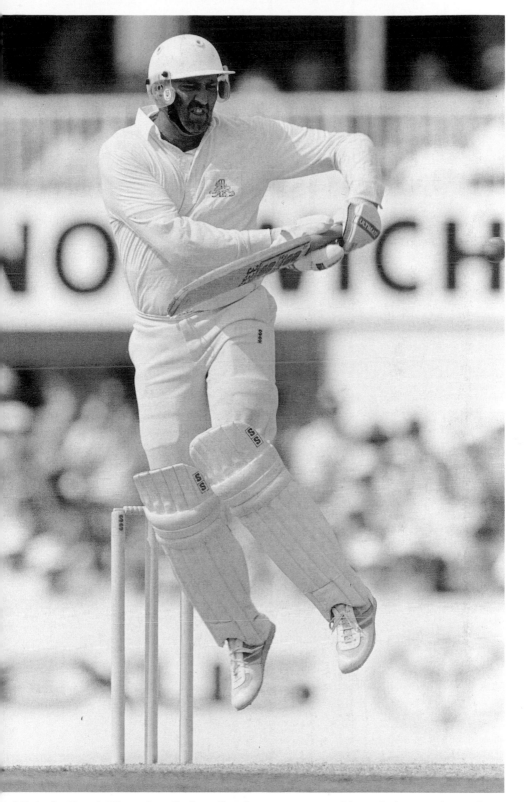

Life in the Fourth Dimension. Graham Gooch came to terms with unstinting pace better than most. Here he deals with Patterson at the Oval, 1991

Below left: The unfathomable Sonny Ramadhin met his Waterloo at Edgbaston. *Below right:* Clive Lloyd: charming and supremely gifted but he made Jardine look a novice! *Foot:* Hero or clown? Brian Close never flinched, even when Holding delivered the 'perfume' ball

Below: Cricket was always an adventure with Keith Miller. Batting or bowling, you *sensed* something was about to happen. *Bottom left & right.* The Lillee–Thomson combination shattered Clive Lloyd's team in 1975–76 and set the big man thinking. The rest of the world would pay for it

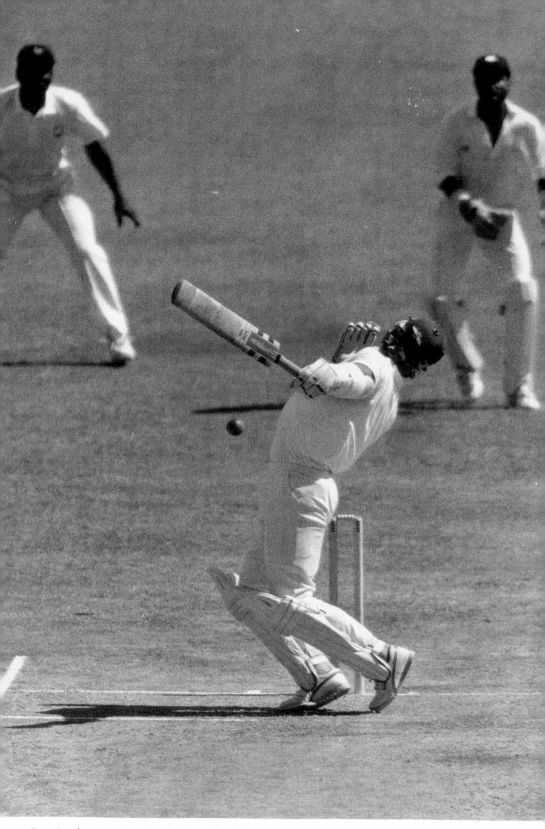

Despite the occasional body blow like this in Antigua 1990, Robin Smith is one of the few
batsmen in the world who *loves* fast bowling

He defies the textbook, looking inside his left arm as he bowls, but Malcolm Marshall took fast bowling into a new dimension

Top: M.J.K. Smith was in good company at Lords in 1972. Bob Massie's astonishing performance bewildered everyone. *Above:* Bob Willis seemed entranced for a good hour after inspiring
this incredible victory at Headingley. The power of self-hypnosis worried some

Below left: Being small in stature was an advantage against pace although Sunil Gavaskar could not understand why. *Below right:* The stumps became almost an irrelevance. Mike Gatting, hit by Marshall in Jamaica, can testify to that

'Who's this old bugger?' they asked, but David Steele had a marvellous series against Lillee and Thomson. This was his England debut at Lords

Hoist by his own petard! Viv did as much as Lloyd to encourage devilish pace. England answered with a black paceman of their own – Devon Malcolm, Jamaica 1990

the innings alongside another seasoned campaigner, Edrich (thirty-nine), were bowled out for 71 and 126. Close's box was cracked by a ball from Roberts! Alan Knott gave Greig a twenty-minute lecture on not giving up the fight. Who was grovelling now? Greig soldiered on, only to be humiliated by Michael Holding who scattered his stumps with a full-length ball before the captain could get his bat down. The bowler was 'hyped'. The air crackled with venom.

Michael's *tour de force* was on an unresponsive pancake of a pitch at the Oval in the last match of the series. Short-pitched bowling was palpably out of the question so the twenty-two-year-old Holding tore England limb from limb by putting the ball up to the bat at lightning velocity. He took 8–92 in the first innings and followed it up with 6–57 from twenty overs in the second. Lloyd describes it as the 'finest fast bowling I have ever witnessed in Test cricket'. Of Holding's fourteen victims, twelve were bowled or leg before.

'I hadn't got the experience to recognize a dead wicket and bowl accordingly. I was young and exuberant and ready to take wickets in any conditions. All I wanted to do was grab the ball and charge in.'

While England were being routed, Amiss on his comeback was putting together a double century. He at least had come to terms with his nightmare, the background to which we have already covered. Edrich, on the other hand, had played his last game for England. Being peppered by four men without a break was not the type of cricket which appealed and he told the chairman of selectors to count him out.

'For more than ten years the West Indies' success has been based on four chaps bowling *at* the batsman. I was glad to get out. At Manchester I told Alec Bedser I couldn't see any point in playing. We'd had the start of it with Lillee and Thomson, but it was getting stupid. I didn't want to be part of it any more.

'Now I'm not involved I can take an objective view. I think an awful lot of damage has been done to Test cricket by Clive Lloyd's attitude. In that 1976 series his quicks bowled eleven overs an hour so each batsman would face five on average and there'd be two balls an over he'd try to play. Add it up and you've got perhaps ten balls an hour from which to try to make runs. It's a joke.

'The West Indies showed their true colours when Graham Gooch's team were about to go 2–0 up in Trinidad on the 1989–90 tour. They took even longer to bowl their overs and got away with a draw. Nobody likes to lose but in the early part of my career you wouldn't resort to those tactics. If you lost, you lost honourably. It's the duty of the captain, in this case Viv Richards, to play fair and show respect for his opponent's ability.

'Winning at all costs won't do the game any favours. Cricket's meant to be a spectacle. We're part of the entertainment business. When you've got 30,000 spectators they don't want to spend all day watching someone walking thirty yards back to his bowling mark then another batsman getting hit. It's a hollow victory if you're hitting the opposition on a regular basis. Clive can boast that he had the most successful team in the world but he did it by intimidation pure and simple. I'm sorry, I don't agree with tactics like that. A lot more balls are being directed at the batsman's head, even in county cricket. It was a much better game to play when I started, and the fast bowlers were just as good if not better. Fred Trueman wasn't slow, Brian Statham, Keith Miller, Alan Davidson and Ray Lindwall were all very difficult to play. Ray summed it up when he said he wouldn't have been in the Australian side if he'd had to bowl bouncers at numbers 8, 9 and 10. He'd be looking to bowl them out, hit the stumps because he was good enough to do it.'

So of course were Holding and Roberts, so is Marshall and so is Curtley Ambrose. That they chose to direct a good percentage of their attack at the guardian of the wickets rather than the wickets may be rooted in something deeper than sport. Caribbean communities are increasingly eager to rid themselves of the images of slavery and servitude which accompanied their arrival on the world's cricketing stage and dogged it for scores of years afterwards; it was not until Frank Worrell took over the captaincy in 1960 that the authorities deemed it in order for the side to be led by a black man.

The appointment of Worrell's predecessor, Gerry Alexander, was splashed against a backdrop of repressed nationalism in which the colonies, championed by Trinidad, demanded self-rule. Nevertheless Worrell, although an infinitely superior cricketer, was passed over for the West Indies tour of India and Pakistan in 1958–59. Black anger was stoked further when Roy Gilchrist, a tearaway fast bowler who epitomized the Caribbean notion of self-assertion for the depressed minority, fell out with his captain and was sent home. Gilchrist, an unruly young man from the Jamaican interior, did not take kindly to being ordered about by a light-skinned captain with an Oxbridge degree. He bowled beamers at the Indians and delivered verbal volleys at Alexander. It was the last we saw of Gilchrist, the forerunner of the all-speed strategy gleefully embraced by Lloyd.

Clive's own upbringing gives us a clue to the source of his driving motivation to see West Indies established as the world's leading power. His mother, Sylvia, was a stickler for discipline and good schooling. She would scan his reports with a steely eye, fully aware that her son spent more time playing games than studying. If the reports did not come up to scratch, games (including cricket) were stamped upon and Clive's pocket money severely reduced. The oft-repeated message was, 'Education is better than silver or gold'. The desire for excellence was encouraged when it emerged that the young Lloyd was no ordinary cricketer. His cousin, Lance Gibbs, urged him to aim high, not to content himself with dreams of representing Guyana, but to go for the ultimate.

Lloyd's crusade was and is bigger than cricket. He is South American by geography but desperately keen for the Caribbean nations to come together as a political, cultural and fiscal unit. There is no such entity as 'West Indies'. It is a cricketing umbrella, no more. In all other sports, the islands (and Guyana) compete at international level in their own right. While not wishing to interfere with that, Clive Lloyd believes there is greater strength in numbers, cricket perhaps acting as the catalyst.

'What we're trying to show the politicians is that regardless of how far apart we are and how diverse in our political instincts and ways of thinking, we can still be one. It's not easy, but we're showing people that we can be a federation, all pulling in the same direction – one currency, one sugar industry, one airline and so on.'

A 'Caribbean' passport would be awarded to heroes rather like New Year honours and this would give the bearer the freedom of the islands. Clive would have little trouble qualifying.

It has to be emphasized that the inventor of four-dimensional fury, while appearing to condone blood-lust in pursuit of his objectives on the cricket field, was also influenced by the amount of grey matter his men had between their ears. A throwback to those echoes of his youth.

'I want people to respect us for our intelligence. If you are outstanding at anything, all you need is a brain to go with it. Mike Tyson had a wonderful talent but not a good brain. Muhammad Ali and Sugar Ray Leonard had good brains and a wonderful talent. That combination is the first thing I look for in a player. I want to see how he reacts in certain situations, whether he has the intelligence to weigh things up, detect changing patterns and react accordingly. If he hasn't got a brain, there's nothing you can develop.'

Quite a chilling prospect. *Premeditated* slaughter. A team of masterminds armed with Scud missiles!

'If you are playing for your country you've got to be strong-willed. I don't think you should hate anyone along the way. We try to get people out, not kill them. That's the spirit we want to pass on to the younger players.'

But what about talk of blood-lust? Dean Jones, the magnificent Australian stroke-maker, likened the West Indian pacemen to sharks. Once one of them tasted blood, the others dived in too, he said. Clive's rationale does not fully address a question he clearly finds uncomfortable.

'The media blow this thing out of proportion. There have always been fast bowlers; people have always been hit. If the wickets were better prepared there wouldn't be so many injuries. You wouldn't expect Becker or Lineker to perform on rough surfaces. We have guys who bowl at 90 miles an hour. They should be treated the same. The batsman has to take better care of himself as well. If a guy's quick you've got to face him whether you like it or not.

'England seem to have this built-in excuse that West Indies are the best in the world, so they're bound to lose. People *expect* them to lose. It hasn't mattered to them. That's the wrong attitude.'

One of the essential prerequisites for the ambitious sportsman is fitness. Even snooker players (some of them at any rate) acknowledge the wisdom of keeping in shape. Rotundity is a less common sight these days on an English cricket field but it has taken the West Indies to set the standard of athletic excellence. Frankly the English approach was put to shame by Clive Lloyd who engaged the tough little Australian rugby league coach, Dennis Waight, to stretch and bend his bowlers into shape during World Series Cricket. The transformation has been noteworthy. Holding says Waight added 30 per cent to his effectiveness. Joel Garner, much looser than his colossal altitude would have you think, continued to stay supple both as a bowler and a gully fieldsman thanks to the influence of the coach.

That is to take nothing away from Bernie Thomas who managed the best he could with largely unenthusiastic clients. English players, no doubt fazed by the dreamy treadmill of day-to-day domestic cricket, have paid less attention to physical fitness than almost any other sportsmen you could name. Under the Graham Gooch/Micky Stewart regime it began to change, but slowly. Lloyd and Waight would look on disbelievingly as England went through the motions, Lloyd in particular.

'Why did it take them so long to cotton on? If you are playing for your country you have a duty to train hard. You couldn't go into a soccer, rugby or basketball team without being fit. It's part of my thinking that a healthy body means a healthy mind. When you're fit you think more clearly and breathe more freely. It's paid off for us. Now the Australians, the Pakistanis and the Indians are all doing the same – even the English.'

Nevertheless it seems unlikely that any cricketing nation will be able to match the Caribbean production line of pace bowlers. In other words West Indies could be the dominant force for the foreseeable future, give or take the odd lull. Why have the islands produced so many world-class speedsters? No one has studied them more closely than Waight.

'They've got the bodies for it. You don't see too many West Indians with huge shoulders or huge thighs. They're well proportioned. The lower part of the back is the important thing. Apart from Ambrose who's a bit leaner, most of the great West Indian fast bowlers have that nice "bunch" as I call it around the backside – a bit of meat. Michael Holding is lean but he has that good muscle definition where it counts. The same's true of Malcolm Marshall. Whites don't have that type of build. Gordon Greenidge isn't a bowler but if you look at him you see how he has the little extra bump in the lower back. It's in their genes and I think it's their greatest asset.

'Joel Garner's another good example. Being 6ft 8in and weighing seventeen stone means he puts an enormous amount of pressure on his lower back when he bowls for long periods. Joel had a great amount of muscle there and big strong thighs so I hardly ever had to work on his back. It's amazing really. Once we started to improve the flexibility I hardly had to help the other bowlers with back troubles either. Yet in England the quicks nearly always seem to have something wrong with their backs . . . Graham Dilley, Neil Foster, Ian Botham.'

Britain being the coldest and most northerly cricketing outpost in the world, where low wickets are the norm rather than the exception, it is too much to hope that England could generate sufficient weaponry to beat West Indies at their own game however many Academies of Fast Bowling were set up. The suppleness of limb simply is not there. While England searches for *one* genuine paceman to inflict the physical and psychological damage which has been a major part of the Caribbean success story, Richie Richardson and the West Indies selectors seem spoiled for choice. This is Lloyd's prognosis:

'Once you get success, the youngsters try to emulate their heroes. Everyone wants to be a fast bowler. Guys are outdoors twelve months of the year swimming and developing their bodies. One day they'll just pick up a ball and have a go at bowling. It just comes naturally. Once we get the television exposure in the Caribbean that cricket lovers get in England and Australia, the standard will go on improving and the number of pacemen will multiply.'

He could be wrong of course. Television will also spread the gospel of basketball, baseball and American football where there are greater riches to be plundered than cricket could match. For impoverished sportsmen the prospect of hopping across the Gulf of Mexico to sell their talents in the USA would be an attractive one. And make no mistake, American TV channels offer wall-to-wall sport, built around the commercials at very low cost. That should test the Caribbean devotion to cricket.

FIVE

The Resistance

'The first half hour is yours, the next five are mine.'
SUNIL GAVASKAR

Robin Smith deliberately kept his head in line with Curtley Ambrose's high kicking express until the last millisecond before swaying out of the way. He smiled to himself as it brushed his nose. An unnecessary risk, but then England's new middle-order star is different from most people. He enjoys looking down the gun barrel. His older brother, Chris, is his closest confidant:

'Robin does that just for the buzz. He is one of the bravest people I've ever met. Probably the only batsman in the world who loves fast bowling. The faster the better. Some are good at playing it but Robin is turned on by it.'

What a blessing it is for England that Robin became an Englishman before South Africa, the country where he was born and brought up, was readmitted into world cricket. Along with his captain, Graham Gooch, and his compatriot, Allan Lamb, he has confronted the West Indies' seemingly endless barrage of pace and proved that it can be handled. He has also proved that if you are strong, patient and brave, there are runs to be had, victories to be chiselled. His 146 against them at Lord's in 1991 was an immense performance, given that Viv Richards was so eager to retain the upper hand after losing the first Test, and that Ambrose was establishing himself as a superior bowler even to Malcolm Marshall. Robin also displayed a knack of building a big innings with only lower-order batsmen for company. Coming in at No. 6 (the position Sobers always favoured) there was the inevitable danger of running out of partners, but it inspired rather than troubled him. It inspired his partners too. Unless it was Gooch driving the pacemen imperiously through extra- cover or 'short-arming' them through mid-wicket, there could have been no more encouraging spectacle for lovers of English cricket than Robin Smith cracking them square off the back foot with such energy and obvious relish. You sense that he cannot wait for the next ball, which is in itself a tribute to his mental wherewithal. Clearly we should not fret when Robin steps into the Fourth Dimension because, strange as it may seem, he is having a great time out there!

He is not, however, as durable as we may think. The conversations he has with himself at the crease are in some ways an echo of the conversations he has had with his brother over the last fifteen or twenty years. Conversations in the back garden in Durban, when they first showed their prowess while playing together for Natal, and conversations on the county circuit with Hampshire. They were never able to share the same dressing-room for England, nor have a mid-wicket conference in the heat of the battle. Chris was rejected after eight Tests with an average of more than 30, and never recalled even though in recent seasons he outscored everyone in domestic cricket except for Gooch and Graeme Hick. Now the chance has gone because he has forsaken English cricket to become Sales Manager for the Western Australian Cricket Association. More is the pity. Not only did his ability as a batsman deserve more recognition, but his psychological insight into the game could have been harnessed for the greater good. He has breathed extra life into his brother: 'I was given average ability with a positive mind. Robin had more ability but less mental strength. A combination of the two of us would have been the best.'

Contrary to popular mythology, Chris did not stake £10,000 on Robin winning fifty England caps, although he wishes he had. He appreciated his brother's natural talents while others were having misgivings during a longer-than-expected acclimatization to Championship cricket. What Chris did say was that if he had £10,000 to spare he would place such a bet. It would not have looked such a promising gamble in the winter of 1990–91 when Robin was having grave difficulties with Bruce Reid's left-arm slant in Australia. The best batsmen in the world have been unhinged by the angle of a left-arm paceman bowling over the wicket. Sobers and Davidson were worth their weight in gold; with more encouragement John Lever might have enjoyed more success at international level; and the Indian Solkar, a moderate performer by Test match standards, penetrated Boycott's defence with disturbing frequency.

Chris Smith went to Sydney to help Robin, examining his technique from behind the nets and attempting to reconstruct his confidence. That was a tall order because his nerve ends had been sandpapered and a string of low scores could not be camouflaged, but considering he had no training in psychology Chris was able to work wonders. That their consultations with each other were undertaken so informally, almost telepathically, is all the more fascinating.

Chris, the more studious of the two, read a whole shelf of books on the subject and persuaded Robin to flick through the odd tome. They gradually evolved their own formula, as Chris explains.

'We focused our minds on big scores. In the past Robin believed that inevitably every so often you had to make a low score and have a lean patch. I told him I disagreed. My belief is that you should keep on making big scores. There's no logical reason to stop just because you've had a run of success. You should be quietly humble in the good times, acknowledging that any ball can get you out even when you've made a hundred. The important thing is to put that hundred behind you the next match. It's history. Take your mind back to square one and score another century. That way you can go on making big scores all the time.

'I became three times the player by getting my thinking right. In my opinion, cricket at the professional level is played 90 per cent in the brain and 10 per cent with raw ability. Yet 100 per cent of players spend 100 per cent of their time practising the 10 per cent. Why?'

The percentage game is amusing. The equation alters depending on whose view you canvass. Alvin Kallicharran, another deep thinker, says it is a 60–40 split in favour of ability whereas Sunil Gavaskar, who was as unperturbed by ferocious pace as Kallicharran, Smith and Gooch, says 50 per cent of cricket is played above the neck. Whatever the formula, the point is the same: coming to terms with the peculiar demands of batting in the 1990s demands an awful lot more than Alec Bedser's beloved net practice. Gooch, as we shall see, gets his mind straight in his own highly individual way, but he is an altogether more placid personality than the hyperactive Robin Smith, for whom the intervals between deliveries rather than the deliveries themselves pose the problem.

'I do all the jumping around to try to maintain concentration. It keeps me loose and light on my feet. When I talk to myself I'm not always aware of what I'm saying but I just know it keeps me going. I try to feed my brain positive information. As the bowler's walking back to his mark and I'm struggling, I try to imagine he's going to bowl a football rather than a cricket ball. It's a game I play in my mind. I try to picture him running up and bowling a juicy half-volley or a short one outside the off-stump which I cut crisply for four. That helps my confidence for the next ball.'

He discovered these tricks from reading a couple of chapters of *Winning Ways* by Rudi Webster, a West Indian psychologist. The book was passed on to him by Chris who became a student of mind games when a motivation consultant in South Africa warned him as an eighteen-year-old that he would never make it in top-class cricket if he did not think right. Robin was persuaded to put in a little homework.

'I'm not normally a great reader but there were several passages about the power of positive thinking which interested me. I sat down and worked it out. It's a lovely game, cricket. An individual game. You can't rely on anyone else; you've got to think about what works for you. The main thing is to visualize success. Technical things you can put right in the nets, mental attitudes you can't.

'There's a long gap between Ambrose delivering one ball and walking back to his mark to deliver another. You have to fill that, and it's an ideal opportunity to concentrate on those methods. Fair enough, you might exhaust yourself that bit quicker but it works for me. I see people out there looking relaxed and wish I could do the same. I'd like not to jump around so much but I don't want to change anything that succeeds.'

Another trick of Robin's is to imagine that the wicket is more than twenty-two yards long and the bowler, consequently, further away than he is. His brain really does seem to work overtime.

'I do it by looking up and down the wicket and convincing myself that it stretches into the distance. It gives me that psychological advantage knowing the ball can't come through so fast if it has further to travel. Against the West Indies it helped me a lot. I'm comfortable with that method. I didn't adopt it in Australia the previous winter and I struggled. It's worked perfectly since but you can never take anything for granted in this game. When things go wrong, tomorrow or next week or next year, I shall review it. You can't keep scoring runs all the time or you'd be averaging 75 not 45. That would be too fantastic for words.'

That remark possibly explains why Chris Smith refers to his brother's mental strength not being what it should be. He sees no reason why Robin should not be averaging 75 in Tests. After all, Bradman exceeded it by a long way.

'I believe hugely that the only bounds your mind knows are the restrictions you put upon it. Obviously you must have the basic talent which Robin has. He ought not to put a ceiling on his ambitions. People who set their targets high and expect more of themselves are normally the ones who achieve it. The difficulty comes when you hit a bad patch as Robin did in Australia. He was suffering a grave loss of confidence. Worse than I've ever seen him. One has to be mentally tough to create a false air of confidence, and tell your mind you've been scoring runs when you haven't.'

Robin isn't like Compton or Botham. You could not tap him on the shoulder and tell him he was in next. He needs to be fully prepared for what lies ahead. He likes to spend three or four minutes on the wicket the day before, working out where the bowler will pitch the ball and rehearsing his shots. Do enough batsmen spend time the previous evening thinking about the bowler? I doubt it. Obviously with flair players like Botham that technique wouldn't work. They respond off the cuff – cricket's great ad-libbers. Botham was one of the players who succumbed meekly to Allan Border's Australians in the English summer of 1989, while Robin Smith was offering one of the few crumbs of comfort to an increasingly bewildered sub-committee of selectors. Although he was later to fall into the habit of playing across the front pad instead of using a straight bat, he made his mark with 143 at Old Trafford out of a total of 260. They were grim days under the lukewarm stewardship of David Gower. As England crumbled 4–0 to surrender the Ashes, and Mark Taylor, Dean Jones and Steve Waugh plundered the attack, Smith must have wondered what on earth he had let himself in for. Mental strength was nice if you could get it but he needed every confidence aid he could lay his hands on.

'I'm also a superstitious person. I have a four-leafed clover on the back of my bat. A real one, stuck on. There are always a couple more in stock for the new bats but I'm not revealing my clover source. I shall continue with that superstition. It's served me well.'

Under the lid of his 'coffin', that utilitarian piece of luggage which has replaced the traditional leather bag, he keeps stickers bearing legends such as 'Think Big' and 'Walk Tall'. Several of the young England players he began with have cottoned on to it. Angus Fraser carried one which read: 'You can only take wickets if you're bowling.' Since he missed most of the 1990 season with injury, that fairly simple truism must have haunted him more than once.

The Smiths are spread across the globe now, but they are a very close family. Robin's wealthy parents spend time in England whenever they can and once Robin became a father the temptation for him to do so was even greater. Chris can see hazards ahead, however.

'Robin's a great father but he mustn't fall into the trap Seve Ballesteros fell into where home life becomes so cushy that he loses his hardness. He must learn how to be loving and gentle at home but flick another switch when he's playing cricket.'

Hardness may come more easily to a South African-born sportsman than it does to an Englishman. The stiff upper lip, the philosophical acceptance of defeat and the refusal to twist the blade when it is inserted are the traits *we* have grown to admire. We do not like rank incompetence although it has a facility for sneaking in when we lower our professional standards. Incompetence and lack of interest plagued England during that 1989 series against Australia, and when some members of the team promptly high-tailed it on a rebel tour to South Africa they could not have left in worse odour. Smith, Jack Russell and Angus Fraser, who had given everything, deserved to be in better company. Border and the Australian manager Bobby Simpson were excellent role models. Their cricket was superior, their thinking sharper and their desire to win formidable. It is an Australian characteristic.

Since the war, England has won sixteen out of ninety-two Ashes Tests. Australia has won more than twice as many. When Gooch led his players to success at Sabina Park in 1990, it was the first time England had beaten West Indies for sixteen years. In between came series defeats at home by India, New Zealand and Pakistan. Even Sri Lanka managed a draw at Lord's, scoring nearly 500 runs in the process. The 1980s were notoriously barren. Home-grown talent was thin on the ground and the game was bedevilled by a *laissez-faire* attitude from the bottom, where cricket at school had largely vanished, to the top, where the administrators had as much sparkle as a wet slag heap and were justifiably referred to by Botham as 'the gin and tonic brigade'. Kerry Packer had arrived precisely because of that prevailing attitude.

When Packer's circus robbed Australia of its best players, Bobby Simpson was called out of retirement in 1977 to knock the new lads into shape. Names like Serjeant, Toohey, Cosier and Rixon suddenly appeared on the scoreboard, although Jeff Thomson was still there. Simpson was forty when he reappeared on the international scene. Using all the wisdom he had gathered over more than fifty Tests, he guided the Australian rookies to a 3–2 series victory over Bishen Bedi's Indians. Defeat in the Caribbean the following year was hardly unexpected but Australia did at least manage to win the third Test in Guyana and Simpson was soon to be given the job of rebuilding his country's cricket through the next decade. His success persuaded Leicestershire to engage him in the post-Gower era. It was not a particularly happy or successful period for him but he had a good opportunity to study the malaise which was turning England into the sick man of world cricket. Simpson is scathing.

'The English sell themselves short. They set a level of satisfaction below their true potential. I've seen it time after time. Players with enormous ability to hit a cricket ball settle for 1,000 runs a season and an average of 30. They've done it all their careers. It's in their make-up. They needed someone to get to them early and tell them how to compile an innings – to tell them what confidence and arrogance means. We've talked about it a lot with the Australians.'

He and Border had their problems, let us be honest. That humiliation against Gower's men in England in 1985 was followed by series defeats by Pakistan, the West Indies, New Zealand and England again. In Taylor, Waugh and Jones however they had uncovered some real nuggets. In the toughest arena of all, the Caribbean, Taylor scored 441 runs against Ambrose, Marshall, Patterson and Walsh, averaging 49, while Waugh topped the averages with 61 from an aggregate of 367. Both scored big centuries in Antigua where Australia won the fifth Test. West Indies won the series, but Simpson had seen the fruits of his labours. Taylor, he says, was always a class player with boundless confidence. Waugh and Jones were not so straightforward.

'We had to stick with Steve for a long time before he came off. Dean we resurrected and persevered with. The good thing is that each of these guys had a kick up the arse on his way through. It made them tougher and taught them to respect the job more. Playing pacemen is a simple game although the English try to complicate it. They lost the fundamentals – if a bloke bowls short play back, and if he bowls well up go forward. So simple. You've got to occupy the crease to build a big innings but it's no use just standing there. You have to push the ball around. Play straight, run hard between the wickets and *want* to win.'

Cricket is replete with stories of players without coruscating talent who became very successful because they turned their minds to it. Likewise there have been enormously gifted ones such as Doug Walters who blossomed now and again but largely flattered to deceive. Something was missing in him which was more than compensated for in John Edrich and Bill Lawry – two 'awkward' left-hand opening bats who resisted more fury than weaker souls (but better bats) could entertain.

Simpson made up for in brainpower what he lacked in elegance. 'If I was in the middle of a bad trot I'd convince myself I was still a good player and I'd had all the failures I was due. I *expected* to make a score in my next innings. With that approach you make the best out of a poor situation. Too many batsmen are negative. When they have a bad run they believe it'll continue, or when they have a good one they think it must end.

'I learned how to harness my concentration at a peak for five seconds each ball. I didn't bother until the ball was about to be bowled. I was a great believer in relaxing until you had to work.'

England's manager Micky Stewart was envious of the Australian ability to occupy the crease when the quicks were rampant. We had all seen what happened when Botham tried to take on the West Indies quartet with the same approach that had triumphed so spectacularly against Australia. His record against them is poor. Says Stewart: 'Winning at Headingley in 1981 was a tremendous individual performance and no one wants to win for his country more than Both, but it isn't such a great victory to snatch it from the jaws of defeat. Better for victory to take shape from day one so that systematically the opposition becomes paralysed. Cricket's a marathon, not a sprint. We've grown up to wallop the ball because of a run chase. In Australia it's not so, despite their macho image. Dean Jones and Steve Waugh have been given more latitude it's true, but Taylor and Marsh are in the same mould as Simpson and Lawry – they'll happily bat for a day and a half. Graham Gooch was a big hitter but he's learned how to build a long innings against the best bowlers in the world.'

He did it first in Barbados, the graveyard of so many hopes and reputations once the Fourth Dimension had been penetrated. Gooch was the only man to stand up to Roberts, Holding, Garner and the ominous Croft in the second innings. His superb 116 was compiled despite the grief which pervaded England's dressing-room after Ken Barrington's death. That was in 1981. Later on the same tour and in extremely hostile conditions he made 153 at Sabina Park, Jamaica. Gooch is one of very few batsmen in the world who can honestly claim to being relatively comfortable when the ball is hurtling towards his throat all day long. Considering he is largely a front-foot player it is even more admirable.

Jamaica nine years later witnessed one of his greatest coups. Gooch was his country's leader by now. Did we applaud him or pity him? Certainly there was precious little cause for optimism when England departed these shores with a hastily reassembled squad following the trouncing by Australia. This time Gower was carrying a briefcase, not a 'coffin'. We would be reading his purple prose in *The Times* although Gooch made a belated and, as it turned out, futile attempt to get him back at the crease when the party reached Barbados.

We would have settled for a draw against one of the *island* teams; that is how low our expectations were. What we got turned the world upside down although it was probably in keeping with one or two other apocalyptic happenings at the start of the decade. Who could have predicted the end of communism and the reunification of the two Germanys? Who would have imagined Mike Tyson presenting his

WEST INDIES v ENGLAND
Jamaica March 1990

WEST INDIES

Greenidge run out	32	—c Hussein b Malcolm	26
Haynes c and b Small	36	—b Malcolm	14
Richardson c Small b Capel	10	—lbw Fraser	25
Best c Russell b Capel	4	—c Gooch b Small	64
Hooper c Capel b Fraser	20	—c Larkins b Small	8
Richards lbw b Malcolm	21	—b Malcolm	37
Dujon not out	19	—b Malcolm	15
Marshall b Fraser	0	—not out	8
Bishop c Larkins b Fraser	0	—c Larkins b Small	3
Walsh b Fraser	6	—b Small	2
Patterson b Fraser	0	—run out	2
Extras	16	—Extras	26
	164		**240**

Bowling: *First Innings* – Fraser 20–8–28–5.
Second Innings – Small 22–6–58–4

ENGLAND

Gooch c Dujon b Patterson	18	—c Greenidge b Bishop	8
Larkins lbw b Bishop	46	—not out	29
Stewart c Best b Bishop	13	—not out	0
Lamb c Hooper b Walsh	132		
Smith c Best b Bishop	57		
Hussein c Dujon b Bishop	13		
Capel c Richardson b Walsh	5		
Russell c Patterson b Walsh	26		
Small lbw b Marshall	4		
Fraser not out	2		
Malcolm lbw b Walsh	0		
Extras	48	—Extras	4
	364		**41**

Bowling: *First Innings* – Bishop 27–5–72–4; Walsh 27–2–4–68–4.
Second Innings – Malcolm 21.3–2–77–4

world heavyweight boxing crown to an unknown called James Buster Douglas? How could the good ship Gooch brave the Caribbean storm and make off with Jamaican gold when the crew was renowned for getting seasick on a millpond? Sheer piracy. They did it thanks to inspired bowling by Fraser, Gladstone Small and Devon Malcolm on an unusually English-type wicket (the groundsman was tarred and feathered) and hours of defiance by Smith, Wayne Larkins and Lamb, who took another magnificent century off them.

There were even better things to come when Viv Richards came to England on his farewell trip the following year. For nearly eight hours the bewhiskered, unsmiling, unflinching England captain was rock steady as the first Test got under way at Headingley. He watched wickets tumble at both ends of his colossal innings of 154 not out. Sometimes he played and missed, sometimes he took charge, but always he stayed. Even when it went dark and the umpires offered him the light.

'I told Derek Pringle we'd do better to keep going. I didn't want the bowlers having a rest and coming back refreshed the next day. While they were tired it was our best chance of building a decent score. It's the only time I've ever turned down the chance to come off against the West Indies!'

At the time we knew it was a *tour de force*. Now that we can stand back, albeit at short range in the context of Test history, we can recognize it as one of the innings of the century. No batsman, not even Bradman during the Bodyline series, was subjected to such hostility for so long. Deadly accurate unbroken hostility on a track Bradman would probably have considered too dodgy to bother with. (The great man was wont to give away his wicket and wait for the next match if conditions were not conducive to century-making.) Gooch's innings moreover established the platform from which he led England to an epoch-making victory over West Indies on English soil. It had not been achieved since Derek Underwood had Sobers and his team-mates in a spin in 1969. Add to that the fact that in scoring 154 out of 252, he contributed 61.6 per cent of the total – the highest proportion ever achieved by an England player. It was not just about batsmanship; it was about standing firm and staying calm in the teeth of an unremitting cyclone, knowing there would be long periods when runs were of secondary importance and could only be gathered at enormous risk. There is probably no other batsman in the world who could have done it. And that includes the West Indians who never had to endure such torment.

What kind of man is this, then? From where does his inner strength derive? Not for Gooch the psychoanalysis or hypnotherapy you will read about in the next chapter. He is bored by and even scornful of external interference. His karma is through physical fitness. Ever since I first met him on the England tour of the West Indies in 1981 he has been dedicated to getting into shape. While others went partying and breakfasted late, Gooch was early to bed and jogging along the beach at sun-up. Now he is obsessive about running, often covering the ten miles from his home to Ilford when Essex are playing there. There is no one else one could imagine lapping the Kensington Oval in Barbados in the noonday heat. Gooch did, shirtless, aware that he would shed pounds in minutes and unconcerned about the ferocity of the Caribbean sun. It is as though through physical exercise he can decelerate the passage of time as well as condition his mind to the challenges ahead. He makes light of the West Indian pacemen he has come to know so well but against whom he had not tasted victory in the ten years of trying until that marvellous March day in Jamaica. He says, 'I don't think it matters much what their names are. Whether it's Holding, Roberts, Garner, Croft or Marshall, Ambrose and the others. They're all marvellous bowlers. If the wicket's doing anything at all they'll steamroller you. [Gooch excepting!]

'I remember facing Ambrose at Edgbaston in 1991 and the batsman at the other end asking if I wanted the sightscreen moving. I said I did, preferably between him and me! You've no idea how much I enjoyed asking the West Indies to follow on at the Oval when Robin's century had helped us to score 400 runs for the first time against their four pace bowlers.

'Personally I've always felt fairly confident against the West Indies. It's a positive attitude. In any game you have to go in believing you're going to do well. If you walk to the wicket thinking you're going to get out, invariably you do, so you have to fill your head with positive things. I didn't have to pinch myself to see if I was dreaming after our win in Jamaica because I've got used to winning with Essex. We play cricket to win whether with county or country. If you play well you can beat anyone. It shouldn't be a foregone conclusion that you're going to lose, even against the West Indies who have dominated world cricket for fifteen years. At the end of it all they're only human.'

If he had not yet graduated to superman status himself, Gooch could not have been far off it. His efforts in the doomed Edgbaston Test deserve mention. Shorn of his most trustworthy lieutenant, Robin Smith, who surprised him by crying off with a finger injury, and deprived of his most successful bowler, Phil DeFreitas, on the day he most needed him, the captain had to do it all on his own. The demands were onerous to put it mildly, but Gooch has sadistic tendencies. Marshall hit form with 4–33 when England were put in first, Gooch holding things together with 45 out of 188. Richie Richardson's century ensured a big first-innings lead for West Indies. Saturday dawned with the tourists on 253–4. By lunch the game had swung back in England's favour, only to be jerked away again.

Gooch picked at his lunch and reflected on the unpalatable aperitif he had been forced to swallow: three gale force overs in fifteen minutes which effectively buried the Test and ruled out any lingering hopes of England's winning the series. He had done well to restrict the West Indies to a modest lead of 104, the last six wickets falling for 39. When England's first two wickets went so quickly to a combination of Dujon behind the stumps and Patterson at his rippling best, the captain had as much chance of survival as a man on a raft over Niagara Falls. You could have sworn that Patterson, the last man out, had lost his leg-stump on purpose: no point in scratching around for a few more runs when he could have a quarter of an hour before the interval to barbecue some English greenhorns. Once more Gooch watched helpless as Hugh Morris and the hopelessly disorientated Michael Atherton deserted him. Lunch at 4–2. What was Gooch supposed to say to Hick over the ham salad? The much-trumpeted arrival on the world stage of the Zimbabwe-born prodigy had been a nightmare. One double-figure score behind him and three ducks. Ambrose could take him out at will. Hick, kept afloat by Gooch's faith in him, departed immediately after the ice-cream, trapped for the umpteenth time by Ambrose in no man's land (5–3). As the ball dribbled from his bat to his wicket, the captain's permanent expression – 'I know I look a miserable sod and I wish I didn't' – never altered. Poor chap had seen it all before. The only way to get a job done properly was to do it himself – again.

He cut Patterson for 4 and glanced him to the fine-leg boundary next ball. Suddenly, at 13–3 it did not look quite so horrific. Gooch was no doubt taking the attack to Patterson in order to take the pressure off Lamb, another out-of-form player against whom he would not hear a word. Class is permanent, he would argue, form is temporary. If ever a man needed help at that time it was Gooch. Establishing himself as the world's premier batsman at thirty-eight was one thing, reviving a cricketing nation which had fallen so disastrously apart until he took charge was something else. When injury took DeFreitas out of the firing line, the captain – who else? – filled in with a little bowling himself and did it more efficiently than Lewis or Richard Illingworth whose job it should have been. While they were profligate, Gooch weighed in with six tidy overs which cost him only eleven runs.

His Saturday had begun earlier than anyone else's. He reported to the ground at 9 a.m. for twenty minutes in the nets with Stewart. After his own fitness workout he led the team warm-up, put his close fielders through their paces, then tackled the not inconsiderable matter of trying to rally his men, bowlers with legs like lead who had to try to find a way of preventing West Indies constructing a massive first-innings lead. Thankfully he did not have to say much. Actions speak loudest and the example Gooch sets to others in every department of his game and preparation is faultless. There followed another face-saving innings of 40 from him, a mixture of watchful defence and controlled aggression in awfully trying circumstances. But once he had fallen to Patterson, bowled through the gate, his shoulders seemed heavier than normal as he made his way slowly back to the pavilion. You wondered for how much longer he could keep shouldering the burden. Since he took over the captaincy in 1990 he had, by the end of the series, scored 2,304 runs in 18 Tests (10 against the West Indies) at an average of 72, almost doubling his previous Test average. The statistics were boosted by his mammoth 333 against India. Dexter, the England chairman, paid him this tribute: 'There is nothing more demanding than captaining the England cricket team. You're under the spotlight for days – months when you're on tour. A football captain only has it for the odd 90 minutes. For Graham to come through all that and blossom into the best batsman in the world at his age has been nothing short of amazing.'

Especially when you consider that he gave up the captaincy of Essex after one year because the responsibility was affecting his batting, and that he asked to be dropped after scoring 11 and 13 in the Old Trafford Test against Australia in 1989. Stewart persuaded him to return for the final Test at the Oval but Alderman had a psychological stranglehold on him and once more he failed with 0 and 10. Gooch seemed the most unlikely contender for the England job when Gower was discarded, but the selectors had no alternative. To the immense relief of all concerned – the four ex-public schoolboys, Dexter, A.C. Smith, Ossie Wheatley and Stewart, and the former toolmaker, Gooch – the marriage between manager and captain became a happy one once they had lived down the ignominy of Australia, a trip which could have seen the back of both of them and which appalled Gooch.

'We lost our pride and dignity at the Sydney Cricket Ground. The England team had become a laughing stock. Our poor bowling exposed our pathetic fielding. This was the worst fielding side I'd ever been in. It was a total disaster. I felt helpless, responsible and embarrassed. I would never have believed that any side I was in charge of could be so inept. It was the worst day of my cricketing life.'

Gower's fly-past put the tin-lid on it. Fortunately Stewart and Gooch, though from diverse backgrounds, bonded well. The manager learned his cricket at the Stuart Surridge School of No Nonsense and the captain had watched Brian Taylor then Keith Fletcher transform Essex from laughing stock to the Liverpool of county cricket. Neither was in the least extrovert, Gooch positively shunning publicity and treating triumph and adversity with the same deadpan countenance. Kipling would have rejoiced. The synergy was no accident, according to Stewart: 'I was aware when we offered Graham the captaincy that our philosophies on life were similar. We dislike defeat. We both believe that enjoyment is being good at what you do so we prepare accordingly. If you fail, you must never say: "If only I'd practised against short-pitched bowling before getting out." You have to eliminate the term "if only". That's not boring. To me and Graham it's pleasurable to get it right. Common sense is what it's all about. If people found it difficult to operate within our policies and enjoy it, then they wouldn't play.'

Serious stuff, but then cricket has become a much more serious business. With the exception of Robin Smith, who could honestly say there was any pleasure in it since Clive Lloyd's decree? The pleasure came when it was over – if you had done well and escaped with your faculties and bones intact. That suited Gooch. He is a serious man. An uncomplicated man who knows what he likes and likes what he knows: his wife and three daughters who take up most of his spare time; West Ham Football Club; the occasional pint, and being fit. 'Have you ever met any sportsman who was a worse player for being fitter and stronger?' he asks. So that was that. When it was suggested to him by his predecessor, Ian Botham, that dawn jogging in the Caribbean was sapping his energy, Gooch snapped back: 'You only know about it 'cos that's the time I pass you on the way home from a party!'

Nothing could have been further from Gooch and Stewart's philosophy than the Botham method of captaincy and way of life. The manager weeps behind his smile if you mention broken beds and buxom blondes or high jinks in herbaceous borders.

'If you're brought up to respect the traditional qualities of the game, it's annoying when something drags it into the gutter. Golf is another great gentlemanly game but its traditional qualities have been well protected. The players run it by themselves. They jump on anyone who steps out of line. We should have handled cricket with the same love and care. I like a drink as much as the next man but to enjoy myself thoroughly and laugh and feel at home in a party, I don't need to be legless. When I wake up in the morning I look forward to the day. So does Graham.'

David Gower does too, but for different reasons these days. Skiing or photo-safaris in Kenya are more likely to consume his winters than cricket, which is an awful shame. His performances against the West Indian quicks have more to commend them than most even though he has not been a great motivator of men. The nadir was not so much the successive whitewashes by the West Indians in 1984 at home and 1986 on tour, but the lamentable collapse of form and spirit when Australia beat England 4–0 in 1989.

Make no mistake, it was desperately sad to watch Holding, Garner, Marshall, Baptiste and/or Davis cutting swathes through the English batting in 1984, but Gower could not be held responsible for leading a touring side which, with the sole exception of Lamb, was far too fragile for its task. Eighteen months later he had the misfortune of trying to cope with an additional whirlwind, Patterson the Jamaican, as well as the brouhaha surrounding Botham. At the peak of his fame, or should I say notoriety, Botham invited more publicity than either he or his agent, Tim Hudson, could manage. Hudson mistakenly believed he could turn his client into a Hollywood film star and Botham gave Hudson his full backing. It was no good squealing when a regiment of gossip columnists and scandalmongers joined the bona fide cricket writers on a truly bizarre excursion. Botham's breaking a bed was headline news. Gower fell into the trap. He was captured on film either pleasure-boating or sunbathing on Caribbean beaches when the more diligent members of his troubled party were at the nets. It bore scant resemblance to highly paid professional sport.

But worse was to come when England capitulated before the nation's very eyes to an Australian side with no pedigree and no reason for believing it had more than an evens chance of winning the Ashes. If anything, England were favourites. That series marked the end of Gower's captaincy. He had been recalled when Gatting fell from grace following allegations that he had cavorted with a waitress at the team's hotel on the rest day of the Trent Bridge Test. Emburey, Chris Cowdrey and Gooch all had a stab at the captaincy in that farcical summer of 1988 before it returned Gower's way a year later. Even then there was confusion. The chairman of selectors wanted Gatting reinstated but the nomination was vetoed by Wheatley, the chairman of the TCCB Cricket Committee.

'Laid-back' is the most popular adjective whenever Gower's approach to cricket comes under scrutiny. If you want the sackcloth and ashes routine when England lose or Gower follows another wide one and is taken at gully, then it is no good looking to him. But if 'laid-back' is meant to imply an emotionless indifference to success or failure, then it is misleading. The fact is that Gower is one of the finest natural talents we have unearthed. Because of his undoubted short-comings as a committed pro – or to put it another way, because he has difficulty concealing the fact that cricket is not the only thing in his life – that talent is wasted. Hampshire fans, sponsors and officials deserve their pound of flesh, but do they really expect him to explode into life at a level of cricket he mastered as a teenager? That is not intended to insult Hampshire, nor to exonerate Gower who is the author of much of his own misfortune – simply to state that provincial rep is not the same after Grand Opera. As Gatting says, 'Some people are born performers. They find it hard to do the mundane stuff in county cricket. David's the perfect example. Put him in a Test arena and he's pure class.'

The West Indians have thought highly of him since his 154 saved the final Test in Jamaica on Botham's tour of 1981. He had become only the fourth Englishman to take a Test century off the toughest attack in the world. The other three were in the same series: Boycott, Peter Willey and Gooch. The list does not grow quickly. To this day only three more players have added their names: Lamb, Graeme Fowler and Robin Smith. Gower also scored 54 at Bridgetown on his first tour to the Caribbean and five more half-centuries against them including 66 each in Trinidad and Barbados and 90 in Antigua on the whitewash tour of 1985–86 when he heavily outscored the rest of the party. On top of that he made 88 not out in a big stand with Gooch in the first Test at Trent Bridge in 1988. That effort – and the rain – combined to deny Viv Richards the chance of a third successive whitewash and prompted singing and dancing in the streets of Nottingham.

Overall against the West Indies, Gower scored 1,149 runs in 19 Tests and averaged 32.8. Not surprising that Richards and his team were delighted to see him excluded from the England team in 1991. What is the relevance, then, of positive thinking in Gower's game and how did it help him to join the Resistance in a decade dominated by black pace? First he takes us back to Sabina Park in March 1981. He was twenty-three when he posted his only century against them. On the final day his self-discipline was so unshakeable that he batted through all three sessions for 84 which for Gower especially was much harder than smashing the same score in a couple of hours.

'I was pumped up for that. I talked to myself a lot to make sure that I was in the right place to do the right thing. I wouldn't like to tell you what I said – most of it is unfit for human consumption. I felt good that day. Sometimes you can walk to the wicket, take guard, stand and look at the bowler and it will feel absolutely right. You haven't done anything consciously different, that's the surprising thing. The next day you can follow the same procedure and everything feels wrong. I've had a few of those.

'It's a tremendously pressurized situation, more so if you're thinking's not quite attuned. Peter Willey and Paul Downton stayed with me for a long time in Jamaica but there's a limit to what you can do to help each other. You have to work it out yourself. In my case it was coping with the ball that slanted across me. A lot of left-handers do nick the ball to the slips when they're having a bad day. At the same time they do also crack a hell of a lot of runs through point and cover. That in effect sums up my career.

'I believe the difference between good and average players is first of all talent, then peace of mind. Sometimes you have it, sometimes you don't. Then it's important to focus correctly, to watch the bowler and watch the ball leaving his hand. It's dangerous to anticipate what Croft or Roberts is going to do. If you're right you've got an extra split second. If you're wrong you've made life difficult for yourself. There's a natural instinct when you've played a lot of quick bowling to think ahead. By that I mean covering an option rather than making up your mind what shot to play before the ball's released.

'You try to teach your body to do the right things instinctively when your eyes tell you. I think you can train your mind to pass on the information more quickly. In other words if Holding bowls you a bouncer you want your instinct to say, "OK, I'm going to watch it; keep my eyes on the ball, bend the knees." If your instinct is to turn your back on it and pray then you're relying on luck and faith in God.'

When Gower led the England team to the West Indies in 1985–86, he decided there was nothing to be lost in adopting a different policy. The mission was well nigh impossible – anyone but a deranged optimist could see that. The captain had been heavily criticized throughout his career for 'going for his shots' when caution was required. He argued that to attack was his natural game (much as Botham did) and that to play the sheet anchor role was unnatural and doomed to failure. Now he was trying to get across to the England players the necessity to go for runs instead of being inhibited by the pacemen. Or, to be more precise, in Gower style he allowed himself to be talked into it by the more forceful members of the party.

'I didn't go so far as to issue orders saying, "You will play shots," but we reasoned that the death ball would come sooner or later. Better to have some runs behind you when it did. Part of the psychology of batting against the West Indies was realizing there was little point hanging around for hours without scoring. We said to ourselves that if there was half a sniff of something to hit we had to have a go at it. If you've batted for three hours and got 20 it's no insurance against a ball that can get you out at any time. You can seldom say you've played yourself in so you might as well have a go.'

It worked up to a point for Gower who made those three half-centuries and came within ten of his century in the last Test which the West Indies won by 240 runs. For the rest it was a spectacular failure. As Botham had already discovered, you took liberties with the West Indian attack at your peril. Willey, the Geordie recruited whenever the going got tough but otherwise ignored, got away with brutal ripostes from time to time but the others let Gower down.

One of the select band of English centurions against the four-frontal West Indies assault, Willey is best known for crashing Croft over gully into the crowd at the Antigua Recreation Ground on his way to three figures. That happened on the 1980–81 trip: 'I can't remember even seeing the ball. Something in the subconscious told me he'd bowled a bouncer. Out went the bat, it hit the middle and went for 6. Nothing preconceived, but the next one was – I ducked. It was obvious what was coming. Croft was the meanest. If he couldn't get you out he'd ping you. His team-mates said he'd bounce his grandmother if he played against her.'

'Send for Will' was the clarion call from Lord's whenever a series against the West Indies beckoned. He played fifteen of his twenty-six Tests against them. You could guarantee that he would not bat an eyelid whatever exploded around him. He was not even overawed when Botham was on the rampage, as Both frequently was on tour. Willey was the one man with whom he would not tangle. One of my most hilarious memories of the 1981 trip was the afternoon in Trinidad when Botham at his most mischievous attempted with unqualified success to toss everyone and their belongings into the pool.

Parched after the havoc he had wrought, he strode over to the poolside bar to order a pina colada and engage the local 'talent' in conversation. Willey, who had escaped the carnage, sneaked up behind and pulled his captain's swim trunks to the floor before he could resist. Beefy spun around in a state of vexation but seeing Willey towering over him, backed off. That was Will for you. Scared of no one.

'I feel sorry for young batsmen coming into the England side knowing they're going to be peppered from the first ball to see if they can handle it. I didn't enjoy playing against the West Indies because we didn't have a great chance of winning. The best we could hope for was a draw. The most worrying time was facing Patterson in Jamaica. The wicket was rough. He was banging them in half way down the wicket at a hell of a speed and some were skidding though at ankle height. That's the only time I started to think about my little daughter and wonder what the hell I was doing there.'

Willey and Lamb, his former Northamptonshire team-mate, were two of the players who agreed to take part in an experiment by Oxford University's Department of Experimental Psychology in 1986. The others were Wayne Larkins and John Lever. The aim was to answer the question which intrigues all cricket enthusiasts – how can a batsman react fast enough to play a sensible shot when the ball is travelling at 90 m.p.h.?

According to Dr Peter McLeod, who carried out the tests, it takes between 200 and 300 thousandths of a second for anyone to pick up visual information about an uncertain event in the outside world and to react appropriately. Cricket clearly carries more uncertainty than baseball for example because of the involvement of a third party – the ground, which helps to determine the speed, direction and height of the ball reaching the unfortunate batsman. Dr McLeod, a keen cricketer who opens the innings 'at low club level' when required, has always been mystified by the way you can hit a ball one day and miss an apparently identical ball the next. He goes on: 'Given that the bowler is trying to make the ball deviate after bouncing, that the ball is an irregular shape, and that the ground is often slightly uneven, the batsmen will frequently face deliveries which change direction unpredictably and reach them in less than 200 thousandths of a second – in other words before they've had time to adjust their stroke. On that basis batting looks impossible. Yet that is absurd because the best players in the world can bat for hours on end without missing a ball.'

Doubts had been cast on laboratory measure-of-reaction times because of this fundamental contradiction. Maybe prolonged practice, high motivation or the mental selection procedures which elevate professional sports persons above the rest of us, had produced cricketers who got into position in under 200 milliseconds? If that were so any scientific attempt to study skilled behaviour would be at best pointless and at worst misleading. Whatever the case, it conjures up wonderful images of white-coated boffins carrying clipboards and endlessly debating the theory of Malcolm Marshall's in-ducker. Dr McLeod, who considered himself fortunate to be getting paid for studying an area of psychology which embraced his favourite hobby, pressed on. He reasoned that facing a cricket ball might not after all come into the category of 'an uncertain event in the outside world'. At least to a seasoned pro it might not.

'It's conceivable that after years of highly motivated practice the flight of the ball becomes such a predictable and salient stimulus for professional cricketers that it can be handled like information about their own body rather than information from the outside world.'

Another thought: since the batsman starts his stroke before the ball bounces (indeed, often holds his bat aloft before it's released), then his reaction is the MODIFICATION of a movement already in progress, rather than the INITIATION of it. This is where our four England men come into the picture. Each faced up to forty deliveries from a bowling machine at fast-medium pace, some short-pitched, some over-pitched and others on a good length. A number of strips of one-centimetre dowelling were placed under the matting wicket, parallel to the line of flight of the ball. A ball landing between the dowels did not deviate; landing on the dowel caused an unpredictable change of direction. As well, some of the short-pitched deliveries landed on a tilted ramp and came through head high. The batsmen, incidentally, were warned in advance about these.

Dr McLeod found no evidence of any adjustment of stroke in less than 190 thousandths of a second after the bounce of the ball. He took a close look at the hook shot too and came to the following conclusion:

'Even at the relatively modest velocity of 65 miles an hour, a bowling speed at which many good batsmen would hook with confidence, it only gave a time window of plus or minus ten milliseconds for the shot to be played. In fact to play it properly the batsman must hit the ball in the meat of the bat, a region not more than 20 centimetres long. Any batsman who plays this shot regularly and successfully against fast-medium bowlers must be judging the time of the arrival of the ball with an accuracy of not less than plus or minus four milliseconds.'

An analysis of high-speed film of Test cricketers batting showed that the reaction time of professional cricketers was in fact no different from that of casual cricketers who would have no chance of resisting the likes of Marshall, Ambrose, Patterson and Walsh. The difference was eventually pinpointed as the 'organization of the motor system that uses the output of the perceptual system'. In layman's terms, Dr McLeod deduced that players like Lamb (there are not many), who have scored six centuries against the most hostile stuff the West Indians could muster, coped with pace by adopting a range of strokes which minimized the danger should the ball change direction. These include playing defensive shots with limp wrists so that the momentum of the ball is absorbed.

The studies and findings of the tests were published in the International Journal of Sports Psychology, but Lamb does not pay them much attention. He is not a great theorist about his art, preferring to let his impulses take over. Apart from a bad summer in 1991, Lamb's performances against the most dominant side in world cricket are impressive – 22 Tests, 1,342 runs, average 34. In 1984 he somehow compiled centuries at Lord's, Headingley and Old Trafford while the rest of the team was annihilated. Not the least of his problems was getting to his target before running out of partners. What distinguishes him from the rest? Why does he play his best innings against the most searching opponents? Lamb is not at all sure. He is, however, a hard man to unnerve and has worked out his own technique.

'Leave it until the last minute before making your movement. Keep your head and body still and never take your eye off the ball. I don't go back and across. Just as important as all that, though, is the determination not to be overawed. I've played with one or two England batsmen who say to themselves, "God these guys are too quick. How are we going to score a run off them?" That's no good. No point going to the wicket if that's what you think. What you have to remember is that you can't play textbook cricket against them because if you get in behind the ball with your elbow well up and ride it, all of a sudden one bounces higher, hits you on the gloves and you're caught behind. Neither can you take them on by hooking every ball. You must keep the scoreboard ticking over and make sure if you get a half-volley or long-hop outside the off-stump that you hit it for 4. You can't afford to let those go. It could be a long time before you get another.'

His trial by fire came in the first Test at Sabina Park in 1986 on the infamous 'corrugated' wicket where Patterson had pulverized his own kind: six men had been carted off to casualty as Patrick reduced Guyana to 19–8 and the Leeward Islands – Richards included – to 78 all out. What chance did England stand? Phil Edmonds, whose occupation-of-the-crease proposal had been laughed off in favour of the 'do or die' approach, recalls Lamb coming in at lunch on the first day.

'He was deathly pale and his legs were shaking. Just as if he'd had a car crash and was in deep shock. Of the 24 balls he'd faced before the break, 22 had been "perfume" balls – Smell the leather.'

The batsman gathered himself heroically and soldiered on to score 49. England, however, were dismissed by tea and psychologically destroyed for the rest of the series when West Indies won in three days.

Lamb is pugnacious to a fault. 'Playing against four quick bowlers all the time is not pleasant, I can tell you. If you can't play short-pitched bowling they find you out very quickly. What we've proved is that the West Indies aren't unbeatable. We tried to get that message across at the start of the 1990 tour and we proved we were right. When you stand up to them, stack a few runs away, you can tell from their eyes that their spirit can be broken. They lose that extra yard, then the field starts to spread out. Suddenly you've only got two slips instead of five which means you've a better chance of getting away with a nick. That's what we hope for. That's what we play for.'

It may be coincidental but three of the world's batsmen who have found effective counters to West Indian speed are around 5 ft 5 in in height – Lamb, Border and Gavaskar. Lamb sees no great significance in it. 'I thought the shorter you were, the harder it was to play short-pitched bowling.' Possibly, but a low centre of gravity is useful when attacking the short ball, as Fredericks and Kallicharran showed against Lillee and Thomson. The shorter you are the smaller the target and the easier it is to get underneath or outside the line of the ball. Gavaskar, whose century at Port of Spain in 1976 was the bedrock of India's match-winning 403 in the fourth innings which convinced Lloyd that speed wins matches and spin does not, believes that altitude is a disadvantage: 'I don't envy the taller blokes. The ball is constantly reaching them at throat height. They had to pitch on a good length to bother me.'

Not many people could bother the world's leading run getter when he set his mind to the task. His record against pace speaks for itself. Gavaskar set the tone when Lloyd's team went to India in 1974–75. West Indies won the series 3–2 but in nine innings, Gavaskar amassed

732 runs at an average of 91.5. It began with a quickfire double century in his home town, Bombay, continued with 107 and 182 not out in Calcutta (he became the first man to score a century in each innings of a Test match three times) and ended with 120 in the fifth Test back in Bombay. By then he had scored ten centuries against the West Indies, far more than anyone else.

When he had a relatively quiet tour of the Caribbean in 1982–83 during which his 147 not out enabled his country to draw in Guyana, Mohinder Amarnath excelled himself with the consistency no other batsman in the world has shown in the face of that four-pronged onslaught – least of all an Englishman on West Indian soil. Amarnath, nicknamed 'Jimmy' by his father who admired most things British, made only two scores under 40. This is how the sequence went: 29, 40 (Jamaica); 58, 117 (Trinidad); 13 (Guyana); 91, 80 (Barbados); 54, 116 (Antigua). Average 66. According to Mihir Bose's *A History of Indian Cricket*, the West Indians agreed with Imran Khan's assessment after the Indian tour of Pakistan earlier the same year that Amarnath was the best player of pace they had seen. His fall from grace was spectacular. Six months later, when Lloyd brought his men to India, Amarnath scored five ducks in the six innings before being dropped. The resistance had gone.

Gavaskar, however, enjoyed a revival just as he was being written off. Marshall and Holding were backed up in particularly deadly form by Davis, Roberts, Daniel and Baptiste. In the first Test Marshall unleashed the dreaded 'perfume ball', Gavaskar's bat flew out of his hand and he gloved a simple catch. He had made seven to add to his first innings 0. He told Vasu Pranjpe, his confidant and the captain of his old club side in Bombay, that he did not see the ball, *or* the point of carrying on in this vein. Pranjpe the sage had the perfect answer: 'Remember how Stan McCabe scored 187 not out by taking the attack to Larwood at Sydney? Why don't you do the same. Fast bowling like this cannot be contained, it has to be counter-attacked.'

He did counter-attack, scoring a vigorous 121 in the next Test at Delhi, 90 in Ahmedabad and 236 not out in Madras. It was his highest Test score and surpassed Bradman's record of twenty-nine Test centuries.

'I always believed in giving the first half-hour to the bowler – the next five were mine. That was my maxim for being an opening bat. It was put into my head by Vasu when I was young. There was no fear when playing the West Indies pacemen. Apprehension yes, because in the first few overs you wonder whether you can cope with the bounce and speed. When the bowlers are fresh and the ball's moving about, you want to feel that your feet are moving too. Then you can remove the sting before you counter-attack.

'Andy Roberts was the number one. You could never relax, even if you'd scored 150. I had two long innings against Andy so I had plenty of time to study him. He threw everything at you but gave nothing away with his facial expression. With most of the others you'd get past 30 and feel you were 99 per cent in charge. Not with Roberts. He put so much into his deliveries he had to put the brakes on to avoid bumping into you. Malcolm Marshall was the nearest thing to Roberts. I was never completely at ease with him, nor with Imran in the early 1980s.

'The most dangerous bowling was Michael Holding's in Jamaica. He went around the wicket bowling beamers and short-pitched deliveries. That was undisguised intimidation rather than an attempt to get you out. It's unfair play too because you can't score from balls flying over your head. I don't begrudge the West Indies their four pacemen. Every team should be selected according to its strengths. The West Indies don't have any quality spinners.

'Batsmen will get on top again, you see. The pendulum is swinging back. I believe good batsmen will always find a way of scoring off fast bowlers as long as their will is strong. Gooch and Lamb have proved what England can do.'

Australia's Allan Border singles out Marshall as his most unwelcome opponent although he says the main preoccupation is not with getting hurt but getting an unplayable ball. 'I would never say I'm happy to receive a blow but if you cop it, you get on with it. You're glad he hasn't got you out. The thing about bowlers of Marshall's quality and pace is that if you give them half a sniff of victory, they're all over you.'

The Australian captain's record since he was beamed into the Fourth Dimension compares favourably with Gooch's, his one-time county colleague at Essex, although Gooch has scored five centuries against the West Indies since 1979–80 alongside Border's two:

'The first time I ever played against the West Indies I couldn't believe what was happening. I felt completely out of my depth. I couldn't imagine I'd ever do anything against them except block the ball and somehow try to keep it out. The idea of scoring boundaries was a joke. I thought I was going through purgatory.' How well he adjusted. Nowadays, he says, he is inured to the ball flying over his head or whistling past his ears.

RECORDS v WEST INDIES SINCE 1979–80

	Tests	Innings	Not outs	Runs	Average	100s	50s	Highest score
Border	26	50	7	1,754	40.79	2	12	126
Gavaskar	11	20	2	745	41.38	3	1	236 no
Gooch	26	51	2	2,197	44.83	5	13	154 no
Gower	19	30	3	1,149	32.80	1	6	154 no
Lamb	22	42	3	1,342	34.41	6	2	132

Another Englishman stood out in this huge spiritual battle against four rampaging speedsters: Geoff Boycott. He has not had to suffer it as long as Gooch and Lamb but his method was as effective as anyone's. Boycott did not desert his principles. Sound defence was the foundation and his back-foot technique gave him ample opportunity to counter-attack square on the off-side. Boycott's century in Antigua in 1981 was a model innings, contrasting as it did with Willey's more savage approach. He would have been devastated to hear the theories propounded by Willey, Gooch, Willis, Botham and seconded by Gower, the captain of the 1984 expedition, that the long-handle method was the only way to resist. He was (almost) speechless when some of the newer members of the Stewart/Gooch school of 1990 threw caution to the wind.

'It's vital when you're defending a big total like 450 to put the accent on defence, not scoring runs. You have to stay there against these boys. Leave things outside the off-stump and be very good at playing the ball off your body around the rib cage where the fast men come at you. Not like Wayne Larkins did in Barbados. After one and half days in the field watching Carlisle Best score 100, he gets out in the first over. That's demoralizing to the rest of the team.'

Boycott of course did that very thing at the same ground nine years earlier when Holding whipped up his sudden frenzy. Holding however is very complimentary. 'He was such a good technical batsman, a very good judge of line and length. He wouldn't play at most balls others would play at. That put pressure back on the bowler because you had to think about control. You had to bowl straight to Boycott. A ball pitched just outside off-stump and moving away would get many batsmen pushing at it. Not Boycott. With him you've wasted all that energy for nothing. You couldn't stray on to his leg-stump either because he was very strong there. You had to be as consistent as he was.

'Gavaskar was a great batsman but when I bowled against him he didn't seem to have the spirit he had years before. In the early 1980s if the wicket had some life in it, he didn't seem to be that interested. Having said that, if Gavaskar didn't want to get out you couldn't get him out. I remember his mammoth innings in Madras. Brilliant. He seemed to be batting with the entire stadium. You couldn't pass the test – you just had to bowl as tightly as possible and hope he'd make a mistake. With other batsmen you know their weaknesses and play on them. Not so with Gavaskar. He just takes charge and you hope he doesn't score too many runs off you. There aren't many batsmen in that category.'

Boycott did not take charge in that sense because, apart from that famous 146 in the 1965 Gillette Cup Final against Surrey, his game was about reducing risk to an absolute minimum. However, rumours that he had no stomach for the heavy artillery were scotched on his last Caribbean tour. Holding has this to say:

'You were never worried about Boycott embarrassing you. I only remember him hooking me once, but he wasn't easy to intimidate. A lot of people said he didn't like fast stuff, didn't want to face Lillee and Thomson, but I never saw him look as if he wanted to back off. Not once.'

Who will ever know the secrets of Boycott's psyche? Even Gavaskar, to whom he has been misleadingly compared, does not begin to comprehend his slavish devotion to batting. Boycott had the same drive and the same desire to collect runs whether he was playing in a Test match or a charity game. Admirable and disquieting at the same time. Gavaskar was not so obsessed:

'First-class matches on tour didn't interest me. I kept my concentration for Tests. I admired Boycott for his single-minded determination. He'd score a Test hundred one day and be at it again on the county circuit the next. Tremendous self-motivation when hardly anyone was watching him. I could never be like that.'

Boycott's former Yorkshire captain, Brian Close, has another expression for single-minded determination.

'Selfishness. You *can* succeed without it. It depends how much the game means to you. To people like Boycott it wasn't as important as his own success. I spent hours telling him what to watch for, how to use his time at the non-striker's end studying the bowler. Watch where his fingers were, where the seam was. He never passed it on. Too jealous of someone learning and becoming better than he was.'

It is well known that cricket to Geoffrey was more than a way of life. It was a reason for living. His success was a badge he wore with immense pride among the working community of South Yorkshire where he insisted on living even after his mother died. Bernie Thomas got to know and respect him as a dedicated professional but was concerned about the chip he had on his shoulder.

'I think it was because his father, who was a miner, had to work twice as hard to keep him on the Yorkshire staff. In those days the ground staff were fifteen–sixteen year olds who got peanuts. His father worked extra shifts to compensate and eventually fell victim to an industrial disease. I had a hell of a go at Geoffrey because he was still living in the cottage where his mother died. He insisted he was going to stay with his community. I told him he was doing a young miner out of a home when he could easily buy his own place.

'He was looking for identification because he couldn't find it among the cricketing fraternity. What he didn't understand was how Colin Cowdrey and Ted Dexter could become captains of England without a similar sacrifice from *their* fathers. He'd say, "My father gave his bloody life so I could play like I do." If he'd concerned himself with playing and getting the captaincy on merit he'd probably have got it. Mind you, I don't think that would have been a good thing.'

Boycott observed one or two rituals designed to sharpen his mental and physical condition before a big match. The first was net practice, as we all know. Away from the nets or the cricket field he was a complete loner, happy with his own company, regarded by the others as a bit of an oddity. 'Sunbathing saps your energy,' he would say when asked why he was never to be found frolicking by the swimming pool. Cheese and tea (not necessarily together) were the dietary choices which occasionally left waiters in a quandary: how to find Earl Grey in Georgetown, Guyana? Where to lay your hand on Farmhouse Cheddar in Bangalore? When Mr Boycott insisted you had to comply. His apparent faddiness over food was partly explained by the spleen operation he had as a teenager. He was worried about possible infections, particularly on the Indian subcontinent, and was frequently omitted from up-country games to lessen the risk.

Another of his favourite foodstuffs was cucumber. Not to eat – to put on his eyes while reclining on his hotel bed. It soothed him, helped him to unwind. At least that was the theory. Calling on Geoffrey when he was 'buried' in his bedroom could be a chastening experience, depending on the time of day. Many a chambermaid or room service waitress had to hide her embarrassment when he answered the door wearing only his customary pyjama tops. Bernie Thomas, who often had to visit players' rooms to dispense tablets or treatment or simply to let them know what time to meet, says he never saw Boycott in a pair of pyjama bottoms.

'I'd ask him what the hell he was doing and he'd mumble something about they'd seen it all before and if they didn't give a damn, he didn't. If I told him to put some trousers on he just said he didn't like wearing them and that was that.'

The top and bottom of Boycott you might say, but for all his off-field eccentricities he proved that even at the age of forty he had an answer to the best and most hostile attack in the world when he toured the Caribbean with Botham's 1980–81 side.

That brings us to another seasoned campaigner from a mining family who never thought he would play for England. Overlooked for years because he represented an unfashionable county and went about his daily business without fuss or fanfare, David Steele was summoned to fill the breach when Lillee and Thomson had the nation on the verge of nervous collapse. Mike Denness had kissed his Test career goodbye after inviting Australia to bat when the 1975 series got under way at Edgbaston. He thought a placid wicket would be even more placid by the time Lillee and Thomson came to use it. Rain ruined his plans; England were beaten by an innings, Gooch collected a 'pair' on his debut and Denness was replaced by Greig. The first thing he had to do was stiffen the middle order, but how?

Steele thought his chance had evaporated when he was passed over for Tony Lewis's tour of India in 1972–73. Having accumulated 1,600 runs and averaged 50 in domestic cricket, he should have had grounds for optimism. But when his Northamptonshire county captain, Jim Watts, put down a fiver that he would be selected, Steele replied, 'Keep your money. Don't waste it on me, mate.' It made him think, though.

'When I looked around the country I realized I was probably as good as anyone else. Frank Hayes and Barry Wood went on that tour and neither of them had scored 1,000 runs in the season. I thought it was the Northants syndrome again. No future for me in Test cricket.'

Over the next three years, Steele established himself as the senior batsman at Northampton. With young players like Larkins, Geoff Cook and Mushtaq coming into the side, he had to be on his toes. His *annus mirabilis* came in 1975, the year he broke through at international level – and his benefit year to boot. The gritty Staffordshire lad with the silver-grey hair, the specs and the front-foot defence, did not get a gentle baptism as England's No. 3. He did not want it. The first problem was finding his way from the dressing-room to the wicket when his moment arrived in the second Test at Lord's:

his visit to the gents toilet was a purely involuntary detour. That navigational hiccup out of the way, he charted his passage to a half-century, defying not only Lillee and Thomson on heat, but also 'Tangles' Max Walker who had been instrumental in the Australian victory at Edgbaston. Steele backed it up with 45 in the second innings; 73 and 92 at Headingley, and 39 and 66 at the Oval. His average for the series was 60 and England drew those remaining three Tests. The style of play was similar to Boycott's – defence first; punish the bad ball. Their personalities had a lot in common, shaped as they were in tough, working-class environments where you had to labour for what you got. Both men brooked no nonsense, stuck to their own way of doing things and derived no pleasure from après-cricket. Drinking in pubs was a waste of time and money – better to do the job you are paid for, then pack your bags and go home. In Steele's household too, cricket was much more than a game.

'If you didn't win, there was no tea. My mother would be at the door asking how I got on. "Lost?" she'd say. "Lost?" as though you weren't allowed to lose. I'd hear my dad chuntering in the kitchen. I'd have to make myself a sandwich. When we won it was nice to have the peace of mind that things would be right at home. I'd be king then. "Cup of tea, our David?" Mum would ask. "Would you like a piece of cake?" Dad would be purring quietly in the corner. He never played sport. Didn't watch me or my brother (John Steele of Leicestershire) very often. In the winter he'd watch Stoke City every home game. In the summer he supported Nelson in the North Staffordshire League, the team Martindale and Sobers played for. He'd say: "I've got my club to watch, you've got your game to play. Carry on." '

Twenty-seven thousand people watched Steele score 50 on his debut at headquarters – roughly five times as big as any audience he had experienced before. He was oblivious.

'I floated out through the Long Room. People were looking at me. I could hear them muttering, "Who's this old grey bugger?" as I walked past. Tommo stood with his hands on his hips. I said, "Good morning Tommo." He said, "Bloody hell, who've we got here, Groucho Marx?"

'I didn't hear the crowd. I always had tunnel vision. Whenever a colleague held up play because someone walked in front of the sightscreen or moved in the crowd I used to ask them why they were looking in that direction. They should have been watching the bowler and the ball in his hand. A herd of elephants could go past and it wouldn't bother me. I hit a 4 early on that morning and the crowd erupted. It sounded a long way off. Beautiful feeling. I loved it, knowing I was in command. I didn't mind Lillee because I could line him up. Tommo was terrible. So were Roberts and Garner when I faced them the following summer.

'My mind was just perfect that year. Clear, cool and sharp. Once I took guard I was in a world of my own. It's the best I've ever felt mentally. Time didn't mean anything.

'What's more, the wickets were great. In Staffordshire I'd grown up on little low seaming wickets with the ball darting all over the place. You had to play on the front foot. It was the same at Northampton. We never had wickets like that one at Lord's. Test tracks were a dream. Never mind Lillee and Thomson, if you got in line it was lovely. Hey, come on, I'll have a bit of this. There was no greater adrenalin than facing the quicks. You'd get a shiver up your back when you knew you were doing the job. I felt I could almost eat the ball I loved it so much!'

England's unlikely hero came within eight runs of a century at Headingley when the command had been issued to score quick runs – an unusual bonus for him. What sticks in his mind most is Alan Knott's belligerent little burst.

'Great cricketer, Alan. He came in and slogged Tommo for 6. He said, "What have I done?" I said, "You've hit him bloody miles." He looked worried: "I shouldn't have done that." I said I wished I'd done it.'

Steele at 33 was at his peak after twelve years in county cricket. His sangfroid when confronted by Lillee and Thomson made you wonder where he had been all these years – it also belied Boycott's warning to Amiss that he would never be a Test player if he played off the front foot. Front-foot batting did not seem to hamper Steele because his eyes were sharp and he could quickly transfer his weight on to the back foot or sway out of line when the ball reared off a length. This despite his glasses. He had an old-fashioned attitude to safety too.

'I loved old gear. I'd had my cricket shoes for ten years – they were like slippers. Couldn't stand anything that cluttered me up, unlike Dennis Amiss. He couldn't believe it when I put on my old gloves. They were going rotten but they felt lovely on the bat. I never wore a thigh pad. Towels were good enough. Roy, the pavilion attendant, came into the dressing-room at Lord's with a marvellous set of towels. I put one of them around my leg. Amiss was getting his gear on. I'd never seen anything like it – chest protector, arm pad. I told him he looked like a knight in armour. I thought this was supposed to be cricket! He said, "Why are you wearing a towel? You're not serious?" I said, "What's wrong with a towel? You're all right, get it down your trousers man. You've got a bat in your hand, you don't need anything else." '

Graham McKenzie had been right when he applauded Greig's decision to go for Steele. The Australian paceman had seen enough of Steele in county cricket to know that the big occasion would not inhibit him. Illingworth silenced the doubters too by declaring, 'If they knock Steeley down, he'll get up again.'

He got up again when West Indies arrived in 1976. And he averaged more than 30 during that torrid series. He made two scores of 40 at the Oval, 64 at Lord's, and 106 in the first Test at Trent Bridge. That was undoubtedly his greatest moment. Brearley was out early and Steele batted for the rest of the day, getting into a rhythm as he calls it.

'You had to get your mind used to long delays knowing that with each over another six balls had gone and they still hadn't got you out. While you're not getting out, you're collecting runs. That's the rhythm. Edrich said he was bored and that's something else you had to fight. Three minutes for a ball to be bowled, it goes past your nose then it's passed all around the field to the bowler again. He goes twenty yards back to his mark while you wait. You get down on your bat, have a fiddle around to see how you're doing – Oh! My back's stiff. Is he coming or what? Oh, here he comes . . . no–ball! Bloody hell. Let's go for a walk. Another long wait. That's concentration for you.

'The last over of that Saturday at Trent Bridge was an eternity. I was on 106 but had cramp in my top hand from holding the bat so tightly for so long. Dickie Bird was moaning: "What's up with you? Get on with the game. Let's get off this field!"

' "I've got cramp, Dick."

' "Cramp? Rub it."

'I did. Wayne Daniel bowled a 9-ball last over. It started at 20 past six and finished at 25 to seven I felt as though I was cracking. Thought I'd never last. That's when the little man inside starts talking to you: "Come on. You've worked bloody hard all day – are you going to give it all away in the last over?" That makes you hang on.'

Lillee joked at the end of the 1975 series that he would 'sort Steeley out' when he got to Australia. 'Are you picking me to go to Australia? That's a compliment. I don't think so!' Steele replied. Alas he was right. He never did go on tour. The selectors convinced themselves that he could not play spin and left him at home for the forthcoming trip to India and the Centenary Test. Steele was annoyed, but grateful to have had the chance to play for England and to score a century against Lloyd's West Indians.

SIX

The Treatment

'In a stunned state Phaedrus began a long series of lateral drifts
that led him into the far orbit of the mind, but he eventually
returned . . .'

ROBERT M. PIRSIG

Jim Laker was a relieved man when Barbados was swamped by
tropical storms in 1947. The twenty-five-year-old finger spinner was
not enjoying his England debut in Gubby Allen's makeshift team.
Sixty-six wickets for Surrey in the 1947 Championship season had not
prepared him for Worrell, Weekes and Walcott on baked clay. He
admitted he was too awestruck to pitch more than three balls an over
where he wanted. Because the batsmen hit them hard, Laker was
uncertain where to pitch the rest. Most un-Lakerlike and fatal for a
slow bowler.

Laker is by no means the only one to have suffered attacks of self-
doubt. When he returned to the West Indies five years later, however,
his trepidation had subsided. He had gained confidence in his ability
and more control of his bowling. The art of spin bowling is more
mentally taxing than pace or seam. By definition a quick bowler has a
larger margin of error. It is possible to be beaten for pace as Boycott
(despite his protestations to the contrary) was by Holding in
Barbados. It is not quite so common to be beaten for *lack* of pace. The
remotest sign of nervousness in a slow bowler is magnified and
ruthlessly exploited by world-class batsmen. He has to be a
psychological colossus to succeed in that company or he compro-
mises his craft (as many have done in recent years) and settles for the
one-paced, flat attack. There have been one or two spectacular
nosedives and several serious cases of 'the yips' where slow bowlers
have got themselves into an emotional tangle and been unable to
release the ball.

Treating that sort of trauma and ensuring that other cricketers are
not afflicted has become an area of growing interest although as yet the

surface has barely been scratched in this country. Australia, as we shall discover, is a veritable breeding ground of psychologists. For the moment let us focus on Birmingham where, by coincidence, three of the most extreme examples of cricketers in crisis came to light and where the application of psychology in sport is being given an extended trial.

Dr Ian Cockerell pressed the right button when he contacted Warwickshire's new chairman, Dennis Amiss, in 1990 proposing a programme of mental preparation to improve the team's performance. Amiss took to the idea, remembering how he had resorted to outside help after his own mental demolition at the hands of Dennis Lillee.

'Within five minutes of him walking into the room, we were all on the same wavelength – our Director of Coaching, Bob Woolmer, the psychologist and me. Dr Cockerell talked about the players setting goals in their lives, having a definite plan for the future and helping each other in discussion after a game. There were lots of ingredients, all positive.'

Positive thinking had been the missing ingredient in Amiss's make-up following the 1974–75 tour to Australia. Never mind oranges, Lillee could have got me out with a watermelon. Discarded now, Amiss began repairing his damaged morale on the county circuit. It was a slow, painstaking rehabilitation which had its reward in the drought year of 1976. West Indies were in town. Tony Greig was having to grovel more than he expected and decided experience would be his saviour in the last Test at the Oval. Was his old buddy Amiss the man? There was a chance to find out when Warwickshire played Sussex at Hove in the NatWest Cup a week before. It looked a good wicket to Amiss.

'When we went out to bat, Greig said to John Snow in a loud voice so that I could hear, "I want you to stick it up Dennis's ears. I want this bugger out!" Snow replied, "Right, skipper," then he let me have the lot. I played it well, got a bit of confidence and finished with 80-odd. A couple of days later Greigy phoned and said he wanted me back for the last Test, how was I feeling? Jill, my wife, who took the call, said, "I think he's ready to take it again now." She knew what I'd been through.'

Jill was right. At a parched Oval without a blade of grass in sight Amiss scored 203 while Michael Holding produced his 14-wicket masterpiece. To much criticism, the revitalized opening bat used his 'back and across' technique, exposing the leg-stump which West Indies were unable to dislodge until Amiss had made his point most forcibly. John Arlott proclaimed that he had achieved little on one of the flattest wickets of all time. That's as maybe. Holding was still bowling like a man possessed, occasionally beating Amiss's bat but failing to undermine his confidence. Fingering the dent Holding had sculptured in the back of his head a few weeks earlier, Amiss kept telling himself, 'Watch the ball. Don't duck, for Christ's sake don't duck!'

So far so good. One major hoop still to be penetrated: the Centenary Test in the cauldron of Melbourne Cricket Ground where those old gunslingers Lillee and Thomson were waiting to renew battle. On arrival Amiss received a letter from Lee Saxon, a psychologist and motivation expert who boasted success with Australian Rules players and surf rowers. Mr Saxon did not beat about the bush. He told Amiss Lillee had a sign over him which he thought he could remove.

'I went to see Lee just before the Test. At the time I didn't have a positive thought in my head about Lillee. Lee told me to keep reminding myself I was a good player and to reject anything negative. I had to stop thinking, "Oh dear. He's going to get me out any minute. What if I get one which seams away and I'm caught behind the wicket again?"

'Instead I had to say to myself: "It's a good pitch and I'm going to do well. If I get a good ball hopefully it'll miss the edge." It did me a lot of good. I'd never approached a game like that before. I even tried some hypnosis. It helped me a lot.'

Sixty thousand Australians were chanting 'Lillee kill Amiss' as he walked out to bat at No. 4. It is a long walk at the MCG. There was plenty of time for Amiss to regurgitate Saxon's words. Lillee's first ball whistled past his nose and dumped him on his backside. The crowd was in uproar. Lillee began his taunting. Amiss was stirred but unshaken. Derek Randall won the Man of the Match award for his marvellous 174 which took England close to their target, but Amiss had climbed his personal Matterhorn in scoring 60.

When Dr Cockerell, a chartered psychologist and lecturer at Birmingham University, came along thirteen years later it is not surprising that Amiss saw the possibilities. He was not sure that mind could conquer matter but he was convinced that mental fine-tuning was bound to improve performance. Warwickshire's captain, Andy Lloyd, was wary of his general manager's ideas. Remember that Lloyd, who did not profess to be a bowler, had spent hours lobbing balls to Amiss at the Edgbaston nets when he was re-examining his modus operandi.

'I thought Dennis was zany. We used to say, "A theory a day makes Dennis play!" He needed it to motivate himself. I was too young to understand. Chris Maynard, who was a wicket-keeper batsman, and I bowled half-volleys which Dennis played back to. It didn't make much sense to me.'

The Doctor's theories and talk-ins made more sense. Warwickshire led the Championship race for most of the 1991 season despite having only one recognizable star, Allan Donald, the South African fast bowler, in their ranks. Had it not been for a grandstand finish from the Gooch-inspired Essex, Andy Lloyd's team would have been hoisting the trophy for the first time in nineteen years. Their encouraging season was not entirely down to Dr Cockerell by any stretch of the imagination, but he helped to get the players believing in themselves. Allan Donald, soon to discover the joys of international cricket which had been denied his compatriots for two decades, was one of those to benefit. Not necessarily from Dr Cockerell's mind games, but from a new sense of purpose which blew through the corridors at Edgbaston. Lloyd used Donald in short bursts all season, preserving his fitness and sharpening his cutting edge. He would take five or six wickets in an innings and still feel as fresh as a daisy. Donald's haul for the season was 86, the second highest in the country. Says his captain:

'Dr Cockerell was a useful part of the back-up team although I think most professionals work out their own methods of preparing for a contest. No matter how good you are, you have to have the confidence to do it. I'm sure the mental part is 50 per cent of the equation.'

There is a danger that the credibility of sports psychologists could be diluted by the number of them plying their trade. During the close season of 1991, Andy Lloyd was approached by Jack Black from Scotland who claimed to be the man behind Liz McColgan's success. 'He may have been right,' said Lloyd, 'but I couldn't help thinking that Liz is the one who gets up in the morning and runs all those miles, not her psychologist.'

Notwithstanding Lloyd's cautious approval of any formalized mental preparation, Warwickshire were the first county to lend an ear. Dr Cockerell was not given a full-time contract but his thoughts have opened a few doors of perception. He says:

'A cricketer, like any other sportsman, needs to be at an optimum level of arousal if he is to give of his best. That is, neither too hyped up nor too laid back. It's only when he's correctly aroused that he takes in the right clues. If a batsman is too aroused his vision is too narrow. He may not be selecting those bits of information which are most relevant. For instance the difference between a top-quality batsman and a tailender is that the better player picks up clues before the ball's bowled. He'll notice how the bowler's running in and holding the ball.'

His explanation makes a nonsense of the 'reflex' theory. Research, he says, has proved that the only time reflexes come into a top batsman's weaponry is when he flings up an arm to protect his head. Otherwise, what we mistake for a 'reflex' shot is in fact a batsman picking up the relevant clues earlier than most mortals and responding in a calculated fashion.

A good part of the psychologist's time was spent with 2nd XI players, notably two spinners whose names we do not need to reveal. Both were concerned about the type of problem which confronted Laker in Barbados – how to maintain the edge against a batsman enabling them to bowl as *they* wished and not as the batsman allowed. A subtle mixture of artistry and illusion is the desired recipe. In other words, the spinner is an actor. Unless he has complete control of the ball, he will of course come unstuck. To an outsider, the very notion of trying to remove a batsman with a ball tossed up in the air must seem absurd. Like trying to pick a lock with a piece of wet string! A baseball batter would be beside himself with glee if a slow pitcher confronted him.

Batsmen usually feel the pressure is off when spinners come on. The temptation to prosper while the sun shines, so to speak, can be enormous. A perfect case in point was Botham in Trinidad in 1981. Viv Richards had him caught in the deep as the England captain completely lost his head. What made it so galling from England's point of view was that Richards came on for that express purpose. Although at moments like these the spinner can pick up cheap wickets, he is also vulnerable to the man with his eye in. A few lusty blows can soon alter the mood and the balance of the match. Ray Illingworth was acutely aware of that.

'Purists might say, "Toss the ball up and make them go for their shots." That's OK until you give away 30 runs in four overs and get taken off. I don't believe in playing that way. I believe in making the batsman play every ball but not letting him score a run. You put the pressure on that way. I'd have a couple of men up close for the bat-pad catch so that after half an hour the batsman's getting worried because he's making no progress. Then he has to get out of the trap. It's a load of rubbish putting people out and hoping he'll hit a full toss down someone's throat. I used to bowl with no one out, challenging the batsman to hit me over the top. Some would try and get caught at mid-on. I got quite a few like that. Kallicharran and Mushtaq were two guys who never got the hang of me. I used to tell Kalli there was no point him trying.'

Fred Titmus gave the ball more air and was less concerned about giving away runs. His précis of the spin bowler's art is fascinating. He employed it longer than anyone.

'I was lucky enough to escape the yips but I can understand how it happens. We always said you didn't need brains to bowl fast. That's a physical thing. Slow bowlers have to have their wits about them all the time and be super-confident because they're playing a game of illusions. It's all about what the batsman *thinks* might happen rather than what does. You have to create something in his mind. The funny thing is you get most wickets with straight balls. You know when you've bowled a good ball as soon as it leaves your hand. Where it goes is immaterial. If the batsman tucks it away it doesn't matter. When he comes down the wicket and hits you back over your head, that's a good sign too. It means he's looking for the big shots and you've got a chance.

'Where you had to be careful was with players who were superb off the back foot like Doug Walters. If you were slightly short he'd murder you. Boycott too. Most of the time he was easy because the ball kept coming back to you. But drop it shorter and he'd punch you through the off-side. There was only a fraction in it.'

Back at Edgbaston, Dr Cockerell, although not a qualified cricket coach, set about rebuilding his young spinners' confidence by teaching them to concentrate on many of the points Titmus makes – principally that it is the bowler who should be in command. He can bowl where he likes, how he likes and when he likes (within reason). The man with the bat can only react.

'When they viewed it like that,' he said, 'the batsman shrank into the distance, metaphorically speaking.'

No such illusions were at hand when Basil Bridge and Roger Harman needed help in the early 1960s. Both were highly-rated young spinners who peaked for one season and vanished into thin air. Harman, a tall, slim left-armer took 136 wickets at a cost of 21 runs for Surrey in 1964 before 'losing it' altogether. Four seasons later he was out of the game. Keith Medlycott from the same county has, sadly, endured similar hardship since being chosen to tour the Caribbean with England in 1990. He was paralysed by lack of confidence and unable to grip the ball properly. He labours under the guidance of Geoff Arnold to recover his touch, but psychotherapy has not been tried.

Basil Bridge's story is bizarre. Even with the benefit of hypnosis, a lasting cure for his chronic loss of form was never discovered. Basil was the proverbial teenage prodigy, making his debut for

Warwickshire at the age of seventeen. He had a vigorous action, a long delivery stride and a twist of the body on the point of release. Illingworth studied him in 1961 when Warwickshire played Yorkshire and told M.J.K. Smith he did not think Basil would ever make it because of his delivery stride. Well, he did, briefly – taking more than 80 wickets in 1959 and 123 in 1961 (average 22.99). He heard, unofficially, that he had been shortlisted for the tour to India and Pakistan under Dexter. Suddenly his world collapsed.

A torn stomach muscle, which had been troubling him for some time but remained undiagnosed, eventually required surgery.

'They removed a ball of muscle tissue the size of an orange. The surgeon who did the operation was on the Warwickshire committee but instead of being encouraged to get back out there and bowl, I had this idea planted in my head that I had to take it easy from now on. It became a big psychological barrier. I couldn't run up and bowl because I was thinking too much about what I was doing.'

The comparatively straightforward job of pitching the ball eluded him. Baffled opponents either played tennis shots to head-high full tosses or watched the ball bounce three times before it reached them. From brilliant young hopeful he had regressed to hopeless novice. Then, by pure fluke, a psychologist turned up at Edgbaston. Dr Heslop was accompanying the New Zealanders on their tour of England. Basil's surgeon asked the hapless bowler if he would like a brief consultation.

'Of course I agreed. Apparently this chap had even performed surgery under hypnosis. He'd hypnotized Peter Parfitt on the phone! Dr Heslop put me in a trance in the secretary's office then I bowled New Zealand out. Took the last four wickets. I was so relaxed it was just like the good old days.'

Unfortunately Basil had a relapse the following day for Warwickshire Seconds against Birmingham Parks. There are not too many hypnotherapists around the local recreation grounds. He had further treatment at a nerve hospital but was forced to give up the game for reasons which still mystify him. Now he is the manager of a car trading business in Harborne although he still plays club cricket for his home village of Studley. Perhaps Dr Cockerell could have helped him – who knows?

Don Wilson had anxious times when he lost the protection and support of Brian Close at Yorkshire. Phil Edmonds, another casualty of the yips, remembers trying to hide his embarrassment when Wilson deliveries were bouncing three times on their way to the batsman.

Edmonds was a supremely gifted left-armer when he arrived in Britain from Lusaka. He had developed as a fourteen-year-old playing men's cricket in Zimbabwe (Rhodesia as it was). Copper miners are tough guys and good players. When he moved to school in England, the home of cricket, he found the standard of play well below his own. Edmonds gained a blue at Fitzwilliam College, Cambridge in his first year as an undergraduate, astonishing his contemporaries with his apparent nonchalance.

'My colleagues asked me if I thought I'd get into the University team. I told them of course. It wasn't meant to be arrogant – just that I'd seen what else was available. I believed I could get anyone out. I just wanted someone to give me the ball and let me bowl.'

One of his early games was against Leicestershire, a developing club containing players like Brian Davison, the big-hitting Rhodesian, and Roger Tolchard. Edmonds went through them without too much difficulty, collecting eleven wickets in the match.

'Apart from Davison, I couldn't believe how bad those guys were. They had an opener called Brian Booth who turned everything down to fine-leg. I got him out, then bowled Davison all ends up. I was under no pressure, I loved it and it came easily.

'Later when I joined Middlesex as part of Mike Brearley's "new broom" I got to realize cricket wasn't as easy as I thought. I looked at the averages and it dawned on me that some of these players could play after all. Booth would have 1,500 runs in a season so he was no mug.'

In his second season at Middlesex, Edmonds burst on to the Test scene with all guns blazing. The 24-year-old took five Australian wickets for 17 in his first twelve overs at Headingley and seemed destined for stardom. It did not quite materialize, despite his marvellous natural ability. Cricket bored him sometimes and he never took batting as seriously as he should have. Edmonds could not convince himself that banal county games were his natural habitat. A few doubts crept into his mind, compounded by his disagreements with Brearley. He now speaks highly of his former captain, but at the time he felt he was being underbowled. He was nicknamed 'Chanel No 5' because, like the expensive perfume, he was used sparingly.

'I began to wonder about my value to the team. If you're not used, you lose a bit of belief in yourself although I wouldn't admit it. Wayne Daniel had a similar problem with the West Indies. He was terrific for us because we gave him the ball and told him he was the main man. Clive Lloyd used to keep him back until the others had done their bit. It's dispiriting for a bowler watching others bowl, the wickets fall, and the ball get older. Wayne was never the same man in Test matches for that reason. Who wants to come on when Amiss is 120 not out and you're a last resort? From wanting the ball you end up *not* wanting it when you get it.

'Then there was the problem of trying too hard to show the captain how wrong he'd been. I'd bowl a rank long-hop and get belted for 4. Because I was so angry with myself I'd take it out on the fielders. "Why the hell didn't you stop that one!" and so on. Blaming someone else for your own mistakes. It's a personality defect.'

Edmonds's Test career went in fits and starts. His most successful period was the visit to India in 1984–85, a tour better remembered for the assassination of Indira Gandhi and of the British Deputy High Commissioner who had entertained the team the night before he was shot. England were led by Gower who was at least spared the task of trying to keep his country's most rumbustious sportsman under control, for Botham had declined to tour. Despite the political distractions and an Indian victory in the first Test in Bombay, England won in Delhi and Madras (where Neil Foster bowled superbly) to take the series 2–1. Edmonds was at his best on unhelpful wickets but had the crowd in stitches in the up-country games.

'I couldn't run in to bowl. The last few paces were all right but I developed a stuttering start for reasons I couldn't work out. I compensated by putting more effort into the follow-through which, perversely, was excellent for giving the ball extra flight.'

The yips got to him good and proper in the intervening years while his England career stuttered as noticeably as his run-up.

'Things got so bad I played for the Middlesex Seconds and couldn't do a thing with the ball. It didn't feel right in my hand. Three balls might be OK but the next three went all over the place. Put me in mind of Don Wilson – and Fred Swarbrook, who also got into an almighty mess. I thought it must be something to do with left-handedness. Perhaps it was right about our brains being on the other side. The problems were all psychological. That's what loss of form is. No point discussing it with anyone because I knew what was wrong. I just had to tell myself to stop being such a prat and sort it out.'

He did, but retired with only thirty-two Test caps to his name to become Chief Executive to a public limited company specializing in leisure activities and kitchenware – odd bedfellows. The Rolls-Royce lifestyle and the smoke-filled boardrooms are appealing but the magic he left on the cricket field.

'Such a mysterious game and such a vital part of the lives of so many.

Seventy million Indians and Pakistanis listen to the BBC World Service just for the cricket. That's why Mike Gatting should have been sacked in Faisalabad for prodding a finger at Shakoor Rana. It tainted our culture in their eyes. Cricket's about fair play, accepting the umpire's decision. Very English. Very important. I didn't appreciate it so much at the time – you never do I guess – but being out there in front of a crowd bowling to Allan Border is a "high". Nothing else in the world exists.'

Gatting made his first Test century on the 1984 tour of India. Border has lost the knack of reaching three figures – Gatting took fifty-five innings to discover it. Inexplicable, considering his obvious abilities and his prolific scoring in the County Championship. He headed the national averages for four years from 1981–84 during which he gathered more than 6,000 runs. The teenage wrist spinner, Sivaramakrishnan, who took 12 wickets in the first Test, held no fears for him, and some questionable umpiring decisions went unchallenged, this time at least. But what was it about Test cricket which drove Gatting into his shell for so long? Many good players disappear into the 'black hole' which exists between Test and county cricket, but Gatting was not one of them. He had several 50s to his name. The boy from Edmonton had a major psychological block.

'For a long time I didn't feel at home in Test surroundings. It was probably my fault as much as anyone else's but it's a big thing getting used to new people – like when you're young and you leave home for the first time. You feel insecure. That's how it was for me once I stepped out of that cosy family feeling of county cricket. In the Test arena there are far better players and a lot of bewildering things going on. I couldn't find the peace of mind I needed.

'The Australians are a lot bolder and more arrogant than we are because they play a higher standard of cricket at an earlier age. They come into a man's world at fourteen. I played a lot in men's teams but I was always "the young boy" as opposed to actually competing with them on level terms. In contrast, a sixteen-year-old Aussie plays first-grade cricket in Sydney which is almost county standard. He gets the mental toughness I lacked. That's why I go out of my way as Middlesex captain to keep in touch with the youngsters. I like to know what they're doing, whether they've got any problems. It's an important part of the game.'

Gatting's breakthrough came in Bombay (136) and was followed by 207 at Madras. The floodgates had opened. He grossed 575 runs in the series and added 527 more when the Australians visited England later the same year. To put that into perspective, Sir Leonard Hutton thought Border's attack the weakest from Australia he had seen.

I said earlier that Australasia was big on sports psychology, and so it is. During the Rugby World Cup in 1991, Michael Lynagh, the Wallabies' winger, was for a time awry with his place-kicking. No worries, as they say. Out came his father, a qualified psychologist from Queensland, to analyse the cerebral fortitude required in applying boot to dead ball. Lynagh's kicking improved immeasurably. Queensland Cricket Club has a *resident* psychotherapist.

When yet another Warwickshire player (what is it about that club?), Bob Willis, was despondent after the Melbourne Centenary Test, again it was an Australian who came to his assistance. Trough of despond could be overstating the case but his performance in the match was listless and thrown into starker relief by Lillee's contrasting heroics. Lillee bowled more than 40 overs on a flat track and took eleven wickets. Says Willis:

'I ran out of puff in Australia's long second innings. I wasn't a very potent force. We'd had the best part of two days in the field and I was like a wet lettuce leaf by the end. Lillee had to bowl virtually non-stop because a couple of bowlers were injured. Incredible effort. Tony Greig had a go at me at a barbecue after the game. Why wasn't I as fit as Lillee? How come he could bowl ten-over stints and me only four? I was clutching at straws for an excuse – it had been a long tour of India, I'd been sick, all that sort of thing. Then I found out the guy whose barbecue we were at, Dr Arthur Jackson, was a hypnotherapist. I went to have a word with him.'

What Willis did not know was that Dr Jackson's list of patients included the world's leading batsman, Viv Richards, and his captain, Clive Lloyd, who was building the most terrifying arsenal of explosives cricket had ever seen. Paradoxically the West Indies had been reduced to a jibbering mass by Lillee and Thomson the previous summer and were sent for succour to Dr Jackson by the former Trinidadian sprinter Mike Agostini, who lived in Sydney and knew of his work. Dr Jackson had studied behavioural medicine since 1971. His first dealings with cricketers involved the New South Wales team, but then came Lloyd and company. Dr Jackson recalls his first encounter with them:

'I'll never forget walking into the West Indies dressing-room in Melbourne. I was the only white face. I didn't presume to intrude in their domain. My job was to reinforce their belief in their own ability and help them to focus their minds in combat. That's crucial in any sport. There's an outdated belief that if you are sufficiently confident in yourself, it will see you through. False premise. In the heat of battle the muscles can tighten, the concentration can drift and the focus of attention be diverted. The willpower theory doesn't apply as often as sports people seem to think. Until we gain access to the things which trouble us, we can't control them, however dogmatic we might be.'

As well as Richards and Lloyd, Dr Jackson also hypnotized Lawrence Rowe and Alvin Kallicharran, the diminutive left-hander who became a close friend of his 'guru' when he returned to play club cricket in Sydney. Kallicharran had withstood the Lillee/Thomson blitz as well as anyone, totalling 450 runs in that 1975–76 tour with an average of 40-plus. Nevertheless his memories are painful ones.

'In every sense it was a horrible, frightening tour. Everyone was shot to pieces. People were so keen to get out of the firing line they were manufacturing injuries. Gordon Greenidge kept having a bad back. No one wanted to open the innings. Viv couldn't come to terms with it until the last two Tests. Then we put him in to open and he played like a man on drugs.'

Richards and Lloyd had first consulted Dr Rudi Webster, a West Indian doctor who lived in Melbourne. Neither he nor Dr Jackson could do anything to prevent a humiliating 4–1 defeat by the Australians which highlighted a trait Lloyd feared was essentially West Indian – lack of 'bottle'. He detected a whiff of cowardice and that appalled him, although Lloyd himself came under fire from Richards and Greenidge for alleged lack of leadership. Kallicharran's colleagues told him he 'must be mad' when he insisted on continuing an unbeaten innings of 50 which had been interrupted when he top-edged Lillee into his face and broke his nose. Kalli, his nose padded with cotton wool, added another dozen runs. More importantly, he overcame any hang-ups about returning to the fray before they had a chance to materialize. As he puts it, 'You have to stop those butterflies in your stomach turning into big birds. If you show the opposition you're terrified, that's the end of your cricket.'

All four, Richards, Rowe, Lloyd and Kallicharran, were hypnotized by Dr Jackson into 'an extreme state of relaxation'. The aim was to focus their attention on the important clues while rejecting peripheral ones when Lillee or Thomson came in to bowl. Hard as it is to imagine Richards requiring hypnotherapy, he became a regular patient.

'Viv was a superb subject. He didn't feel in any way threatened by the process, but immersed himself in it completely. We've kept in close contact since. He sent me a letter not long after his first treatment saying it had given him much more confidence against spin bowlers. Until he had the therapy he was never at ease.'

So what exactly was Dr Jackson's value? In what practical ways could hypnotherapy help a batsman? This was his message to Richards and the others:

'I tried to get him to think of two fields of vision, the wide angle and the narrow angle. The wide would take in everything the batsman sees from the crease – how the field is set, the boundaries, the direction of the wind, the sightscreen, the crowd. The narrow focus would take in only the bowler and the ball in his hand. The batsman in control needs to be able to switch from one angle to the other and back again like an automatic camera. When he's anxious he can get stuck in one mode. It's no good focusing on the ball leaving the hand so intensely that you miss the wider view of it swinging in the air.'

Willis, sceptical to begin with, agreed to a session of hypnosis. It was the turning point of his life: 'Just like somebody putting a key in your ear and unwinding all the stress and problems you'd had in your mind on a long and very tiring tour. Fantastic feeling – much better than drink.'

Dr Jackson taught him to relax, which was a heck of an achievement – Willis was an habitually bad sleeper on tour, awake at first light staring at the ceiling in a shared hotel room which was too hot or too cold or too close to the tradesman's entrance or the main highway. Then came the fitness programme. At first England's premier fast bowler could not manage five minutes a day without getting out of breath. 'My stamina was sadly lacking. That's why I was well and truly spent in the Centenary Test. I couldn't cope with 40-degree temperatures every day.'

Gradually he made himself fit and with the fitness came an improvement in his mental approach – precisely what Dennis Waight was preaching to the West Indies players. 'While under hypnosis I would picture myself running in well, bowling well and avoiding no-balls. "Visualizing" became a way of preparing for the day ahead.'

Dr Jackson made him a series of sound tapes to take back to England. He is keen to encourage self-hypnosis, and to dispel a few myths about the subject.

'Hypnosis is one of the best ways of treating anxiety and repro-gramming the mind. Its use on stage as a form of entertainment has aroused public suspicion but most of their beliefs are wrong. The idea of someone being put into a trance during which they're unaware of anything around them couldn't be further from the truth.

'Bob and Viv and the others would be in a beautiful state. Relaxed and aware of what I was saying to them. These ideas about clicking your fingers and making people cluck like chickens are nonsense. All we're doing is gaining access to the databank system that everyone has filed away in his or her subconscious. All our patterns of behaviour over the years are stored there — fear, anxiety, self-esteem, depression etc. It's very hard to get access to them. Only 8 per cent of the population have a *high* degree of hypnotizability. Bob Willis and Viv Richards come into that category. Elite athletes come well up the list because they have the ability to lose themselves completely while they're competing. Bob was down on confidence when he came to me. The stamina work helped him to sleep. Many sportsmen have restless nights before the event. Bob stopped worrying about things and began to accept himself as an all-right guy. He hadn't before.'

Up to the mid-1960s psychology in sport was regarded as the icing on the cake. Then it became apparent to go-ahead sections of the sporting world that it accounted for a good size of the cake. A Professor Nerose from Tokyo University was asked to find an explanation for the poor performance of the Japanese team at the Rome Olympics in 1960. Eighty per cent of them confessed they were struck by stagefright when they first walked into the stadium. Only 20 per cent had developed any psychological techniques to deal with the pressure of performing. Since then every Japanese team has been tutored in self-hypnosis, although the results, as far as we know, are not appreciably different.

Willis, like Amiss, was incapacitated by what is known in the profession as 'negative self-talk'. That is to say feeding negative thoughts into their subconscious before or during a critical moment in their performance. It might be fear of dropping a catch which is on its way towards you; fear of being dismissed early in an innings, or, as in Willis's case, concern about bowling no-balls or losing the rhythm of his run-up. According to Dr Jackson it's a downward spiral.

'The old saying, "Think bad, feel bad" is true all through life. Worrying about things going wrong becomes a self-fulfilling prophecy. All the problems you fear start to happen. Instead of being a world-class strike bowler, Bob was in danger of becoming pedestrian and losing his wicket-taking ability.'

Willis will not mind my saying he was an ungainly athlete at the best of times. He cherishes Frank Keating's description in the *Guardian*: 'A 1914 biplane tied up with elastic bands trying vainly to take off.' Inevitably his 6ft 3in frame would creak at the joints but it took Dr Jackson to point out one major physical discrepancy.

'It wasn't until I talked about the mechanics of breathing that I realized that at the actual moment of delivering the ball I held my breath rather than exhaled. I had my teeth clenched and my lungs full, which was completely wrong. It puts the body under much more strain if all your effort is kept in rather than released with a Jimmy Connors grunt. Making the adjustment wasn't difficult. Once I'd thought it through it came naturally.'

Controlled breathing is a well-recognized way of relieving stress. Bernie Thomas, who spent several years helping Willis to improve his flexibility, recommends closing each nostril in turn and breathing in and out deeply through the other. It ought to make valium superfluous! Breathing from the abdomen rather than the chest is reckoned to be even more salutary. It is widely practised in the East as a means of achieving tranquillity and transcending earthly distractions. D.T. Suzuki, the late professor of Buddhist Philosophy at Otani University in Kyoto, says in his *Studies in Zen*:

> Some primitive people were once visited by an American scientist and when they were told that Western people think with their heads, the primitive people thought that the Americans were all crazy. They said, 'We think with the abdomen!' People in China and Japan, when some difficult problems come up, often say, 'Think with your abdomen,' or simply, 'Ask your belly.'

One or two bellies in the English game could have been called into question before cricket became more athletic with the advent of limited overs. Unless they were fielding close to the wicket, it would have been difficult to place Colin Milburn, David Shepherd and, with the best will in the world, Colin Cowdrey. Darts players and Sumo wrestlers aside, English cricketers, until the Graham Gooch/Micky Stewart era, were among the unfittest sportsmen in the world. Still there is a belief in some quarters that cricket is too much of a gentleman's relish to sink to the trivialities of the training ground. And that despite the success of the West Indies, who are an advert for the all-round advantages of physical fitness. Even Viv Richards was a fanatic and he did not do a lot of running between the wickets! As a former gymnast, Bernie Thomas attached more value to loosening exercises than running. Fitness, he argues, must relate to what you want it for. Walking upstairs on his hands was relevant to Bernie's sporting aspirations but might not have done much for Ian Botham's away swinger.

There is no disputing the logic though that sloppiness too readily transmits itself from the body to the mind. Being overweight at best betrays a character weakness, at worst a dereliction of duty. In a highly paid professional sportsman it is hard to forgive although it clearly suited Botham's psyche to be beefy. There were times nonetheless when he was quite fat. This decreased his mobility as well as contributing to the back problems which took much of the sting out of his bowling. Gross over-bowling did not help, either. Dennis Waight tried to work on Botham at Somerset but found him less of a natural trainer than his team-mate and great friend Viv Richards. Waight knew the best way to *encourage* someone to eat and drink was to tell him not to. Instead he advised moderation. There was nothing wrong with a couple of pints a day as long as it stopped there. Moderation not being one of the great all-rounder's natural instincts, it was an uncomfortable discipline.

As indeed restricting Branston Pickle would be to Mike Gatting! The former England captain was jettisoned and left on the sidelines along with Botham, Gower and several others because his appetite for extra-curricular activities had, in the establishment's view, diverted his attention from the task in hand. Gatting, the supreme professional whose batting at last began to fulfil its potential, was part of England's losing brigade – a demoralized collection of cricketers with a defeatist attitude fashioned by years of defeat. The level of expectancy was pitifully low. Furthermore defeat did not appear to hurt and, according to Stewart, getting out of the side was more difficult than getting into it! He avoided the phrase 'Good-time Charlies' but it could not have been far from his lips when he surveyed the wreckage. Stewart, it must be remembered, was fortunate to fall into the job of England manager when both Ray Illingworth and David Brown rejected it because of its toothless bulldog undertones. Some would say he was even more fortunate to keep it after successive débâcles against Australia. He rode the storms and attempted to impose a new discipline, a new sense of patriotism, a more professional outlook.

'When you say the word cricket in England, more often than not it means beer. The average local club in this country provides the stage for a good social time. That's how our cricketers were introduced to the game. Anywhere else in the world the only thing that matters is a 22-yard strip of turf. Some clubs in Australia don't even have a bar. In the West Indies it's worse. They have diabolical grounds and outfields but thousands of people still love their cricket. To get a game there or in Australia you need ability. In England you can get a game every day of the week without an ounce of ability in your body.

'We provide thousands with huge enjoyment and that shouldn't change. What we need to change is the balance. We should get more enjoyment from achieving sporting excellence than from having a good time.

'We have the talent in this country. There are 600 clubs in Surrey and over a thousand in Yorkshire but all the talented cricketers play in a forest of mediocrity. Seventy-five per cent of English club players are forced to play below their level.

'In order to compete internationally we have to change our thinking right from the earliest age. The traditional English player weighs 16 stone and likes a few pints. Tremendous – but absolutely nothing to do with successful cricket. It's a myth that we're a great cricketing nation, but it's about time we were. We've hardly ever made the best use of our talent.'

As they lined up for the 1992 World Cup in Australia, England were extremely well prepared physically after long sessions at John Brewer's Lilleshall fitness centre, but lagging behind the host nation in mental preparation. Said Brewer:

'Micky Stewart daren't ask for a psychology consultant in England because people would laugh at him. In Australia they laughed because he hadn't brought one.'

The man who was chairman of selectors, unpaid, for seventeen years, finds those sentiments absurd. Alec Bedser is of course very much of the old school, a working-class lad who played for Surrey when the Oval was a cockney oasis of cricket and thousands would take the tram ride from Peckham for a 6d day out.

Bedser does not suffer fools gladly, neither does he have much truck with modern theories. For him cricket was and is a straightforward game. Hard but simple at the same time.

'This Dexter–Stewart–Gooch thing is a lot of bullshit. Ted gets £20,000 a year for a job I did without pay. Micky gets £30,000 and a car and there's a whole bunch of players like David Gower who get a Test salary whether they're in the team or not. If people get rewarded for doing nothing they get spoiled. Why bother to stretch themselves? We knew if we didn't play well we didn't get picked for the next match – and if we didn't get picked, we didn't get paid. I don't care two hoots for motivation techniques and psychotherapy. There's something wrong with you if you need outside help when you're chosen for your country. That's all the motivation I needed.'

Match money applied to county and Test cricket. Some players had insurance schemes to cover them in case of injury but many, like Godfrey Evans, would go to great lengths to avoid injuries and mask them when they happened. Evans specialized in standing up to fast-medium bowlers like Bedser because he preferred to attack and get batsmen out rather than stand back and keep down the byes. It increased the risk of injury.

'You'll see old wicket-keepers with fingers all over the place. They played when their fingers were broken. Bind them up tightly and carry on – that was the way. I used to put lots of binding on my fingers. It was tough work standing up to Alec.'

Nothing unusual in the older generation believing things were better in their day and their scepticism about the benefits of hypnotherapy is to be expected. Denis Compton would not waste time analysing his every move because the very act of doing so would remove the spontaneity from what for him was a spontaneous business. As Mike Brearley intones, 'If a centipede were to analyse its actions every time it put one foot in front of the other, it would never get anywhere.' It is possible that Brearley's presence at Headingley in 1981 enabled Botham to unchain his brain and savage the Australian attack, but such a suggestion is anathema to Bedser for whom success in cricket and life was achieved by the sweat of his brow.

'It's nonsense for people to suggest that Botham played an innings like that because of Brearley. Botham knew it was all or nothing. Lillee bowled like an idiot to Dilley and allowed him to get 50. It makes me wonder about Lillee. Why did he keep bowling outside the off-stump? After that Botham succeeded because he was a fine cricketer. No one said the same to me in 1953 when Len Hutton won the Ashes. All you hear about is Trevor Bailey staying put at Lord's with Willie Watson and what a good job Hutton did. What about me? I took 39 wickets in the series and yet when it came to Sportsman of the Year I came third behind Bailey who spent five hours getting 78 in a single innings. The year before in Australia I got 30 wickets at 16 runs apiece. That's an average of seven wickets each Test in two series against the best in the world. Len Hutton never even gave me a mention in his speeches. If it hadn't been for me he wouldn't have won the Ashes. I bowled 280 overs and never broke down once – not like bowlers today.'

Willis still broke down after his consultations with Dr Jackson. The biggest disappointment was having to return home from the 1980 tour of the West Indies. However, hypnotherapy had transformed his attitude to training. Instead of bowling four or five overs at full pace and petering out fast, Willis was now potent in 10-over spells which made him a much more testing proposition. He says:

'The mickey's still taken out of cricketers training by the Fred Truemans and Alec Bedsers who insist they used to bowl themselves fit. That's garbage. In every other sport, the level of attainment has gone up and up. There's no reason why cricket should be any different. Fred and Alec only ever played 3-day county matches, all at the same pace. They never came on in one-day matches and bowled fifteen yorkers off the last 18 balls while batsmen are trying to slog them out of the ground. It's crazy saying they were fitter in their day just because they bowled 600 overs a season. They were fit for bowling but not much else.'

And so to Leeds in 1981. Before Botham's 'scientific slog' as Brearley describes it, many of England's players had checked out of their hotels and apparently out of Test cricket. Willis was one of them. He had not even been selected for the game. Bedser informed him that Brearley did not want any fitness doubts for such a vital match in which the newly reinstated captain was anxious to bring the series level at one all. Willis, who had pulled out of Warwickshire's match because of an attack of flu, explained that he was deliberately missing the county game to preserve his energy for this third Test. The chairman of selectors had to move fast to intercept Mike Hendrick's invitation to play in the Test before it could reach him at Derbyshire. Australia reached 401–9 declared in their first innings, Willis bowling respectably but without penetration for figures of 0–72 off 30 overs. Seasons during which he knew he was an automatic choice because England had no alternative strike bowlers now seemed to be coming to an end.

'I was bowling for my England life in the second innings. I'd played one of the self-hypnosis tapes to myself and was in the optimum state of readiness. There were no great tactics about it. The turning point came when I changed ends after telling Mike I was too old to bowl up the hill. Two wickets went before lunch and from 50-odd for 2 they were 68–6. The rest was fate. It's a performance I can't really explain. I've bowled better and done nothing.'

On an unreal afternoon which had the nation gripped, Willis, now 32, achieved his life's best 8–43 in only 15 overs and one ball. During that performance and its immediate aftermath, several of those close to him noticed that Willis was behaving strangely. Brearley was one of them, although he was accustomed to the bowler's habit of disappearing into a world of his own.

'Bob Taylor and I tried to talk to him between wickets or at the end of an over, but it was difficult to keep up with him as he loped away with those long strides of his. He seemed more than normally fazed. We didn't feel we were getting through.'

Dr Jackson, watching the match on television in Sydney, had the notion he must have been in a trance. 'He told me afterwards he had just been letting things happen with consummate ease.'

Willis himself surprised the nation with a post-match television interview in which he gave the impression that he had just lost a war instead of winning a Test match. 'I was angry at certain sections of the press who wrote us off as no-hopers.'

Bernie Thomas, who knew the player as well as anyone, did not see anger in his eyes, but a blankness which worried him.

'Everyone at Headingley will tell you Bob was like a zombie for forty minutes after that game. So much so that I'd have sworn he was drugged. I know he wasn't, and that concerned me even more. What do we really know about hypnosis? Whether Bob's condition was a reaction to the game or a result of self-hypnosis I don't know. What I do know is that hypnosis can affect people in many ways. I once had a very bright girl working with me as a student physiotherapist. She was way ahead of her peers until she got involved with a stage hypnotist for some reason. She became very scruffy and unkempt after that and never passed another exam. Personally, I'm afraid of hypnosis.'

ENGLAND v AUSTRALIA
Headingley 1981

AUSTRALIA – SECOND INNINGS

Dyson	c Taylor b Willis	34
Wood	c Taylor b Botham	10
T. Chappell	c Taylor b Willis	8
Hughes	c Botham b Willis	0
Yallop	c Gatting b Willis	0
Border	b Old	0
Marsh	c Dilley b Willis	4
Bright	b Willis	19
Lawson	c Taylor b Willis	1
Lillee	c Gatting b Willis	17
Alderman	not out	0
	Extras	18
	Total	111

Bowling: Willis 15.1–1–3–43–8; Old 9–1–21–1; Botham 7–3–14–1
England won by 18 runs

Freud used hypnosis in his early days but abandoned it in favour of psychoanalysis, not necessarily because of any profound suspicion but because it was directed more towards a symptom than the whole person. It might cure vertigo and arachnophobia or persuade the patient to give up smoking, but its reach would be limited. That is a view shared by Brearley himself. The former England captain is now a qualified psychotherapist and analyst who occasionally has sportsmen referred to him. It was a different story on the England tour of Australia in 1978–79 when Brearley, who captained his country to a crushing 5–1 win, found himself personally shipwrecked by the pace of Rodney Hogg. Australia were chronically weakened by World Series Cricket but, as so often happens, an exceptional player emerged from nowhere. Some have greatness thrust upon them. It happened with Botham and it happened with Hogg. His series tally of 41 wickets at 12 runs each was a remarkable record. He was, sadly for Australia, rather let down by his batsmen.

Brearley, aware that some of his contemporaries deemed him below Test quality as a batsman, was having sleepless nights about a calamitous start to the series. In six innings he had managed only 37 runs. England had won the first two Tests but lost the third at Melbourne. Sydney would be crucial. Something had to be done. The physician could not heal himself because, for one thing, he was not yet a qualified physician.

'I was desperate. Tense and lacking in self-confidence. Bob Willis enthused about Dr Jackson and I thought there was nothing to lose. I went for hypnotherapy but I wasn't a deep-trance subject. I didn't get into the full hypnotic state. I was just very relaxed. If someone had opened the door I'd have noticed.'

Dr Jackson opened a different door, putting the England captain more in touch with his better qualities as an opening batsman, while ignoring the negative aspects. 'He admitted his fears and pressures. We talked frankly about a fear of failure. Even an extrovert like Botham has a fear of failure. It comes from the desire to do well for your country and be well thought of.'

While he was widely acknowledged as a shrewd and deep-thinking captain, Brearley knew that a string of bad scores would reload the guns constantly aimed at his head. He was grateful to Willis for putting him in touch with Dr Jackson.

'I found it very helpful. He diagnosed my problems before the hypnosis then invited me to imagine confronting the bowler – Hogg or Hurst in this case – and visualize my body moving in anticipation as they came in to bowl. It was important to get the body feeling right, important to visualize the activity which was unnerving me. I've conducted psychotherapy on sports people since but I've done it my way without hypnosis.'

There was an immediate improvement in Brearley's form. He scored 17 in the first innings at Sydney, but topped it with his first half-century in the second. 'I felt better, more relaxed, but it's hard to quantify the extent to which therapy helped. In the same way it would be impossible to quantify the relevance of my reappearance to Botham's performances in 1981. It's possible they might not have been quite so likely to happen if I hadn't been there – who knows?' Despite his vested interest in the subject of psychology, Brearley is by no means convinced that professional psychotherapists should be given carte blanche to exercise their powers in sport. Interfering with a player's train of thought and method of preparation, even if it appears faulty, could, he suggests, do more harm than good.

Other players to have benefited from Dr Jackson's techniques, however, include Greg Chappell, who tried hypnosis after the inevitable bad spell and got back into the groove in New Zealand. According to the doctor, Chappell was exhausting himself by playing matches in his head before they happened – taking visualization to damaging extremes.

The New Zealand opener John Wright also sought help. Says Dr Jackson:

'A delightfully laid-back personality until he's on the field and then he gets so intense that his skills are hampered. He falls for the negative self-talk which is perhaps not surprising as an opening bat with 90-mile-an-hour deliveries coming at him. John was talking himself out of form more than into it. His mind went walkabout when he was anxious, which is true of many sportsmen.

'What we did was get him to face the situation he was afraid of and stay with it in his mind. Imagine a large, hostile crowd, a bouncy wicket and a West Indian paceman. Then he measured his fear on a scale up to 100. Once he felt his heart beating fast, his sweat glands working and disorientation setting in, I wanted him to read what we call the "fear thermometer". If the imagined reading was very high, we took him to a quieter place in his mind before reintroducing him to the arena. Then the fear level drops. In real life he could confront the situation better. His mind was saying: "I know how to deal with this now."'

The cue Dr Jackson asked Wright to use was the word 'calm', to be uttered five times as he exhaled. It enabled the batsman to narrow his focus of concentration for several seconds at the critical moment before the bowler began his approach. 'In between deliveries when John was in close-up on the television the commentators would ask, "I wonder what Wright's thinking about out there?" I knew. I could see him saying it: "Calm, calm." '

It is a word which existed only in the dictionary as far as England's most idiosyncratic cricketer of the second half of the century is concerned. Alan Knott merits that title because he played the game his own intuitive way with scant regard for coaching manuals or the advice of others. It is not that he was scornful or truculent but supremely aware of his own strengths and shortcomings. He was also way ahead of his time when it came to stretching his mental faculties. Knott devised his own methods of keeping wicket which would have purists like Bob Taylor wincing, but brought him 269 victims in 95 Tests. Often he would take a catch with one hand when the textbook stipulated two. When batting he would bring his top hand behind the handle of the bat to deal with steeply lifting balls from the pacemen and, maddeningly for slow left-arm bowlers on a turning wicket, he would get away with calculated chip shots over mid-wicket. His use of the sweep was an education. Brearley recalls his sweeping fifteen consecutive balls from Edmonds and John Emburey without mis-hitting: 'He has told me that if he sets his mind to it he can sweep virtually any ball, with the possible exception of the low full toss. His secret is to keep his head still and not try to hit the ball too hard.'

The originality of his attacking strokes helped to turn him into a genuine all-rounder who was in his element bailing his county out of a crisis in the No. 7 position. He scored over 4,000 Test runs and averaged 32. Knott is not given the credit he deserves for being an all-rounder but then, as the *Evening Standard* correspondent, John Thicknesse, points out, wicket-keepers seldom are. John followed Knott's career closely with Kent and England and penned this marvellous testimonial:

'Small, perky, as alert as a cat, he was unmistakable from the furthest corner of the ground, whether crouching low beside the stumps or poised wide-eyed in front of them, as alive to the possibilities of misadventure as a boy playing French cricket on a bumpy lawn. His fanaticism for health and fitness, manifest on the field by innumerable little exercises during breaks of play, and off it by faddiness in what he ate, stemmed from a fear of losing his agility.'

Curiously enough, for all his callisthenics, Knott could not run or throw a ball. This became most apparent in a game at the Adelaide

Oval. Taylor had taken a turn behind the stumps and Knott was put out to graze near the boundary. He could not hide forever and when the ball eventually found him there were hoots of derision from spectators and team-mates alike as he ran in and threw three times before getting the ball back to Taylor. That cameo aside, Knott is an excellent example of what this book is about – the power of positive thinking. Long before psychotherapists turned their attention to cricket, he had (typically) worked out his own programme. This is the side of Alan Knott few will have heard before:

'I trained my mind to accept pressure and even demand it. When the pressure wasn't on I only got average scores and I wasn't at my best behind the stumps. You have to approach the game in the most realistic way possible. If I was facing Dennis Lillee for example I'd be telling myself that my judgement had to be just right to cope with the one that moves away or nips back. I wouldn't be taking the negative view and praying he didn't bowl a great ball which I'd nick to the slips. That never came into my thinking. They call it visualization these days but I was lucky that I could do it instinctively. I didn't need any outside help.

'I've heard stories of Olympic teams being made to train while the noise of the crowd in the stadium is played to them at full blast. I used to do something similar but without sound effects. I'd dream I was in the cricket stadium in Calcutta or Melbourne in front of 100,000 people. Then I'd wake up and feel I was actually there. I could smell the atmosphere. It was *real*. I recreated it just by dozing off in a chair. There can't be any better way of preparing yourself mentally for what's to come. All those things affect you – sights, sounds, smells.'

What a wonderful gift it is to be able to transport yourself to the other side of the world without leaving your armchair – and to programme your mind to replay 'videos' while you sleep. But then Knott was unique. He never enjoyed a quiet day because he wanted to play against the world's best bowlers and batsmen all the time.

'You have to think that way. Others were relieved when Lillee or Thomson couldn't play. I was disappointed. Nothing better than taking the sting out of a fast bowler. The best way of demoralizing him wasn't to blast him around the ground but defend soundly. Let him roar in and throw everything at you then watch you kill the ball stone dead with soft-hands. That's the most demoralizing thing of all.'

New Zealand's greatest bowler – and indeed one of the world's greatest ever – was Sir Richard Hadlee. Only two things ever got to him. One was Ian Botham, his lifelong rival and (as he saw it) potential usurper. The other was a hypodermic needle. The physio at Trent

Bridge would not dream of suggesting an injection unless it was a matter of life or death. It would have taken the SAS to hold Hadlee down.

His aversion had something to do with fear and something to do with disrespect for the mechanics of medicine. He believed that his well-honed body was quite capable of looking after itself thank you very much. Almost inconceivable then that he should be prostrate in intensive care, concealed under a Spaghetti Junction of wires and tubes. The man who bowled 3,460.4 overs in Test cricket and became the biggest wicket-taker in the world went to death's door and back six months after hanging up his size tens.

Sir Richard's retirement plans were unhinged in the most awful fashion at Dunedin in February 1991. He had barely taken his seat as a guest commentator for NZTV when his heart thundered into overdrive. From an athletic fifty beats a minute, his pulse soared to three hundred for no apparent reason. Hadlee was unconscious. Fortunately help was speedily at hand and he was on his way to hospital within minutes. He says, 'If I'd been up country or at the wheel of my car, that would have been the end. I'm very fortunate to be here at all.'

To the batsmen he haunted and the team-mates he inspired it was a mystery that someone so young and fit could have heart problems. Even more bewildering when it emerged that Hadlee had carried his disability for the whole of his thirty-nine years. He was born with Wolf Parkinson-White syndrome, a congenital abnormality affecting the pathways which conduct the heart's electrical stimulation. In other words, his heart rate could have leapt into the stratosphere at any moment. 'I shudder now when I think of all the times I asked him to bowl a couple of overs more,' says Clive Rice, his captain for so many successful years at Nottinghamshire.

Wolf Parkinson-White syndrome can surface at any time in a person's life, or never at all. In Hadlee's case there had been possible warnings as long ago as 1983. Although he was convinced he had heart trouble, the anxiety coincided with a period of mental turmoil which could well have concealed the underlying truth. The first irregularity was at a festival match in Rotorua, New Zealand when very soon after the start he was helped off in a complete daze. He could not see properly and his head was spinning. This is his version of what happened next:

'Over the following few days I seemed to have lost the will to do anything. Normally I run a dozen laps of the local park but now I couldn't manage one. The most terrifying part was going to bed at night with severe chest pains, convinced that I wouldn't see the morning. I was preoccupied with thoughts of death.'

A chance encounter with Grahame Felton, a motivation expert at the Christchurch Institute of Management, helped Hadlee through what appeared to be a nervous breakdown. He went on to even greater feats – inspiring New Zealand to their first victory against England on English soil; single-handedly destroying their batting at Christchurch six months later, and becoming the only cricketer in modern times to achieve the double of 100 wickets and 1,000 runs in an English season. Sir Richard and his wife, Karen, however, now believe that the chest pains were as real as the palpitations he frequently imagined. Says Karen, 'Richard used to feel his heart fluttering when he was batting but never mentioned it at the time because he thought it must be adrenalin.'

Clive Rice recalls several occasions when Hadlee was not merely tired but 'washed up' after an innings. Indeed he had to be carried to the dressing-room and revived after steering Nottinghamshire to a Cup victory over Lancashire. 'It's astonishing that he survived as well as he did at the highest level,' says Rice, 'and equally remarkable that his heart gave out almost as soon as he began to take things easy. Maybe it got used to the stimulus.'

Hadlee agonized for many weeks after his collapse over the question of open heart surgery, a complicated business in his case where a bypass machine would temporarily take over the functions of the heart and lungs. It was a tough decision but in the end a decision which took itself. The drugs he had been prescribed were so powerful that he could seldom complete a full day's work for his new employers, the Bank of New Zealand. Neither did the drugs offer him 100 per cent insurance against another attack.

Hadlee was off the life-support machine and reading a newspaper within two days of the operation. He also kept alongside his bed the motivation card he carried in his cricket bag. As Karen says, 'He loves targets and that was the biggest one yet.'

The card had been compiled in conjunction with Grahame Felton. Some discover faith; Hadlee had discovered the might of mind over matter, which is a faith of sorts. His recovery from mental collapse is the most vivid example of psychotherapy in any sport, let alone cricket. Whether or not his heart defect contributed to what Hadlee prefers to call the 'deep depression' which plagued him is difficult to know. It undoubtedly contributed to the deterioration in his physical well-being that culminated in his operation, but he also betrayed the classic symptoms of a nervous breakdown.

'I became terribly neurotic at home, incessantly polishing trophies, straightening pictures on the wall and picking up dead flies off the carpet. Karen and the family were very concerned about my state of health. The odd day was a little brighter, but the majority were black. Mum brought it home to me when she said that if I didn't slow down I mightn't be around much longer.'

Clive Rice was one of the few callers permitted to talk to him during this period. Karen had put a block on all telephone calls but she allowed him to take this one from Johannesburg. Rice recalls, 'Richard sounded awful. I hardly recognized his voice. It was as though he didn't even have the confidence to talk.'

Felton not only effected a transformation in Hadlee which the doctors could not achieve, he actually spurred him on to more success in the last five years of his career than the all-rounder ever imagined possible. It astonished those who proclaimed he was past his best. Among their rude awakenings was a dazzling 15-wicket haul by Hadlee against Australia at Brisbane in 1985. He took 9–52 off 23.4 overs and 6–71 from 28.5.

'Grahame gave me a recipe for life which I wrote on a card and carried in my cricket bag everywhere. I remember looking at it in the dressing-room at Brisbane. The card got so worn out I had to rewrite it twice. It all started with a three-hour session at my local club,

AUSTRALIA v NEW ZEALAND
First Test: Brisbane 1985

AUSTRALIA

Wessels lbw b Hadlee	70	—c Brown b Chatfield	3
Hilditch c Chatfield b Hadlee	0	—c Chatfield b Hadlee	12
Boon c Corey b Hadlee	31	—c Smith b Chatfield	1
Border c Edgar b Hadlee	1	—not out	152
Ritchie c M. Crowe b Hadlee	8	—c Corey b Snedden	20
Phillips b Hadlee	34	—b Hadlee	3
Matthews b Hadlee	2	—c Corey b Hadlee	115
Lawson c Hadlee b Brown	8	—c Brown b Chatfield	7
McDermott c Corey b Hadlee	9	—c and b Hadlee	5
Gilbert not out	0	—c Chatfield b Hadlee	10
Holland c Brown b Hadlee	0	—b Hadlee	0
Extras	16	—Extras	6
Total	179	—Total	333

Bowling: Hadlee 23.4–4–52–9 Hadlee 28.5–9–71–6

Canterbury, when Grahame met the team. The benefits that came out of that first talk were unbelievable and the timing from my point of view was uncanny. I wasn't seeking the kind of help he was offering but it was soon obvious that it was exactly what I needed. When he discovered I was going through traumas he asked if I'd be his guinea pig. I said I would. It's not easy to recapture the mood of that session. It was intense. Grahame's message came across to me so forcibly it was like suddenly seeing the light.'

Naturally enough there are similarities between what Felton preached to Hadlee and Dr Jackson preached to Willis, but it did not involve hypnosis. Hadlee being a more methodical and clinically efficient person, it is unlikely that he would have been as responsive as Willis on the hypnotist's couch. He was, however, highly responsive to the trigger words suggested by his motivator.

'*Simulation* was a keyword. It meant putting myself back into a situation in which I last enjoyed success. I might for instance be playing at Old Trafford. I'd tell myself I did pretty well the last time I played there, taking five wickets or scoring 70 runs. With Grahame's help I learned to play back those successes in my mind, not as a spectator, but going through the actions again. I would recreate the day in question and everything about it – the weather, the crowd, the state of the game and whatever was occupying my mind outside and inside the game at that particular time.

'I'd then progress to *visualization*, what I wanted to happen this time. No one can control the actions of the other people but I could condition myself to react in ways which would minimize their effectiveness. I could be playing against Middlesex for instance and I'd remember that the last time I faced Norman Cowans, he got me out. Now I'd convince myself that it wouldn't happen again. Turning that around to positive thinking, I'd say to myself, "When Cowans bowls to me tomorrow, I will stay at the crease and when he's finished his bowling spell, I'll still be batting." It works if you believe it strongly enough.

'Grahame explained that my mind was better than a computer and controlled every single thing I did. The brain could be programmed to behave positively. Once it did, the body would react accordingly. All straightforward points, but unless someone spells them out, they'd slip away unnoticed.

'*Belief* was another crucial factor. During my illness I'd begun to doubt my ability, which was stupid. I only had to think back over what I'd achieved to restore my confidence. Lack of confidence is a passport to failure, as I'd seen with New Zealand cricketers for years. Whenever they took on England or Australia, they *knew* they would get beaten. Once you're in that frame of mind you might as well give up.

'*Targets* were already an essential part of my life. Grahame emphasized the importance of wanting to prove myself better than the opposition – not occasionally but every time. Beating the opponent became a driving ambition. Often the opponent was Botham. I had a fixation about it. He was the only one I had to beat, whether in wickets or runs. In the 1984 series in New Zealand I beat him easily on wickets but he edged me out on runs. I turned that series into a personal duel. It was part of the positive thinking programme. In the team talk before the first Test I told the players to pick a rival from the England team and try to outdo him through the series. Our two opening bats took Tavaré and Smith or Fowler, I took Botham, Ian Smith took Bob Taylor, and so on. At the end of the three Tests we compared performances with our opposite numbers. Invariably we beat them with ease. If we each won our personal battle we were bound to win the match.

'*Wanting* to achieve was the next stage. Desire for success had never been a problem to me – quite the opposite. I probably drive people mad with it. Grahame reinforced that part of my mental attitude as well. Winning Test matches or the Open golf, or Wimbledon or any major event, isn't necessarily about the man or woman with most talent. The winners are those who know how to maximize it. They want to win so badly that they do.

'Everyone has a tape recorder inside him. Like any other tape recorder, you can press the rewind button and relive the good times. The bad ones you must erase. If anything negative comes into your mind, cast it out. Another one of my adopted catch phrases was never get tired, just *pleasantly weary*. If you tell yourself you're shattered you will be.

'And to finish with, a phrase which summed up my whole attitude: *winning is being happy with your own performance*, even though someone might have performed better than you. As long as I knew I had given 100 per cent it didn't matter so much if I didn't quite achieve what I was after.'

Ten days into his guinea-pig course, Hadlee was feeling better. The desire to resume his career came back. Once that happened, everything else fell into place. The headaches subsided; the dizziness had gone; the chest pains were a thing of the past – or so he thought.

Like Willis, Hadlee could not wait for his retirement as it drew nearer. He said before the last Test between England and New

Zealand at Edgbaston in 1990, 'People expect you to perform like a machine, to go on day after day. What they forget is that machines break down too. The bits wear out. I'm not doing badly for an old man but I'll be glad when it's all over.'

You might have forgiven Methuselah those sentiments – even Ronald Reagan who was still running the world's most powerful nation well beyond his three score years and ten. But neither, according to the records, ever delivered 25 overs from the pavilion end on a cold Thursday in April with two men and a dog in attendance. Having run nearly 1,000 miles in his first-class career while whistling down 21,115 deliveries, Hadlee deserved a rest. Perhaps Rice is right that his body was not ready for the chemical change imposed by retirement. There are, sadly, endless cases of active middle-aged people dying soon after they retire. Thankfully the world's leading wicket-taker survived his triple bypass surgery.

'It took ten weeks to get over it, and those five months on medication before the operation were a real struggle, but it's a small price to pay to get your health back. Grahame's teachings serve me well in business now. I still need focus and direction – I still need to top up the positive attitude when things go badly. The funny thing is that part of my work with the bank is talking to staff about motivation techniques. I guess I've become a mini Grahame Felton!'

If it is right that through positive thinking, Hadlee overcame, or at least delayed the effects of a physical disability which was waiting to strike him down, then mind had achieved a spectacular victory over matter.

Index